A TEACHER'S GUIDE TO

Vocabulary
Development

Across the Day

A TEACHER'S GUIDE TO

Grades K–3

Tanya S. Wright

Vocabulary

Development

Across THE Day

series editor
Katie Wood Ray

Heinemann • Portsmouth, NH

Heinemann

361 Hanover Street

Portsmouth, NH 03801–3912

www.heinemann.com

Offices and agents throughout the world

The author and publisher wish to thank those who have generously given permission to reprint borrowed material:

Cover and interior pages from *Hello Autumn!* Copyright © 2017 Shelley Rotner. All Rights Reserved. Used by permission of Holiday House Publishing, Inc.

Interior photographs: page 18, © Tim Platt / Getty Images; page 24, © Monkey Business Images / Shutterstock; page 49, © Monkey Business Images / Shutterstock; page 50, © Houghton Mifflin Harcourt / HIP; page 63, © Wavebreak3 / Adobe Stock Images; page 70, © American Images Inc / Digital Vision / Getty Images / HIP; page 79, © Cascoly / Alamy / HIP; page 79, © Houghton Mifflin Harcourt / HIP; page 79, © Thitisan / Shutterstock / HIP; page 79, © Stocktrek Images / Getty Images / HIP; page 79, © Iusubov nizami / Shutterstock HIP; page 79, © Elena Elisseeva / Cutcaster / HIP; page 79, © Michael Blann / Digital Vision / Getty Images / HIP; page 79, © Ariel Skelley / Blend Images / Corbis / HIP; page 79, © J. Luke / PhotoLink / Photodisc / Getty Images / HIP; page 79, © Snaprender / Alamy / HIP; page 79, © Gk-6mt / iStock / Getty Images / HIP; page 79, © Fototi photography / Shutterstock / HIP; page 92, © FatCamera / E+ / Getty Images / HIP; page 106, © Monkey Business Images / Shutterstock; page 108, © Aflo Co., Ltd. / Alamy Stock Photo

Library of Congress Cataloging-in-Publication Data

Names: Wright, Tanya S., author.

Title: A teacher's guide to vocabulary development across the day / Tanya S. Wright.

Description: Portsmouth, NH : Heinemann, [2020] | Series: The classroom essentials series | Includes bibliographical references.

Identifiers: LCCN 2020017743 | ISBN 9780325112770

Subjects: LCSH: Language arts (Early childhood) | Language arts (Elementary) | Vocabulary—Study and teaching (Early childhood) | Vocabulary—Study and teaching (Elementary).

Classification: LCC LB1139.5.L35 W75 2020 | DDC 372.6/044—dc23

LC record available at https://lccn.loc.gov/2020017743

Editor: Katie Wood Ray

Production: Hilary Goff

Cover and interior designs: Vita Lane

Photography: Sherry Day

Videography: Dennis Doyle and Paul Tomasyan

Typesetter: Vita Lane

Manufacturing: Steve Bernier

Printed in the United States of America on acid-free paper

1 2 3 4 5 6 7 8 9 10 CGB 25 24 23 22 21 20

September 2020 Printing

Six

For my parents,
who encouraged my love of
literacy and learning, and for Will,
for his unwavering support.

T. S. W.

Book Map

3 Vocabulary Development During Read-Alouds 28

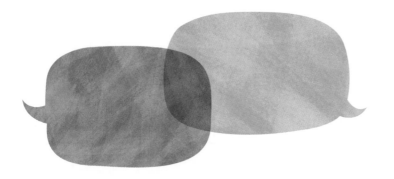

4 Vocabulary Development During Content-Area Learning 54

About the Online Resources

This Classroom Essentials book includes seven videos in its online resources that show teachers supporting children's vocabulary development across the day. Here's what you will see:

▶	
Video 3.1	Teachers offer child-friendly explanations of vocabulary in context. (Whole Class)
Video 3.2	Revisiting important vocabulary after the read-aloud. (Whole Class)
Video 4.1	Exploring words that represent important concepts for content-area learning. (Whole Class)
Video 4.2	Sentence stems help children use new vocabulary in authentic ways. (Small Group)
Video 5.1	Using context clues to figure out an unknown word. (Whole Class)
Video 5.2	Using word parts you know to figure out an unknown word. (Whole Class)
Video 5.3	A teacher previews words before children read a selection from *Mercy Watson*. (Small Group)

Thank you to the faculty and staff at Paddock Elementary School for graciously hosting us in their classrooms to capture this video.

HOW TO ACCESS ONLINE RESOURCES

To access online resources for *A Teacher's Guide to Vocabulary Development Across the Day*:

1. Go to **http://hein.pub /vocabdevelopment-login**.

2. Log in with your username and password. If you do not already have an account with Heinemann, you will need to create an account.

3. On the Welcome page, choose **"Click here to register an Online Resource."**

4. Register your product by entering the code: **VOCABDAY** (be sure to read and check the acknowledgment box under the keycode).

5. Once you have registered your product, it will appear alphabetically in your account list of **My Online Resources.**

Note: When returning to Heinemann.com to access your previously registered products, simply log into your Heinemann account and click on **"View my registered Online Resources."**

1

Setting the Stage

The more words he knew the more clearly he could share
with the world what he was thinking, feeling, and dreaming.

The Word Collector by Peter H. Reynolds

One of the joys of being a parent or teacher of young children is hearing them use new words to communicate. Children's mispronunciations and misinterpretations often lead to delightful stories that become family lore. One of my family's favorites happened when my oldest daughter was five years old. I found her at bedtime lying on her front with her knees curled under her body in what looked like child's pose. When I suggested that she did not look like she was in a comfortable position for actually falling asleep, she told me, "I'm a turtle, and I'm not trying to sleep, Mommy. I'm being a noc-turtle." Once I finished trying not to laugh, I realized that she had been watching a TV show about *nocturnal* animals earlier that day. While she clearly had some misunderstandings about this new word, based on how it was pronounced and her prior knowledge about turtles, she tried immediately to use and apply this new word, *nocturnal*, in a way that pertained to her own life.

We are similarly delighted when children learn and use new words at school. A kindergarten class had been learning the names of different types of clouds and how they predict different weather conditions. One day after school as they waited for the bus, the principal overheard the children debating whether the clouds in the sky were *cumulus* or *cumulonimbus*! They were concerned that if the clouds were *cumulonimbus* clouds (i.e., storm clouds), then their baseball practice would be canceled. The children were actively applying both the new ideas—and the words they had learned to describe these ideas—to important events in their own lives.

Young children love to learn and use new words as they discuss, read about, and write about ideas, as they learn to describe and explain their world, and as they play. In this book, we will explore how vocabulary instruction in the early grades of school can support this type of useful and meaningful word learning for young children.

Before we get started, the first thing we need to do is think about what we mean by the term *vocabulary*. Sometimes, teachers use the term *vocabulary* to mean "sight word vocabulary" or words that students recognize automatically as they read. But in this book, our focus will be on teaching word meanings and not on automatic word recognition. After all, young children know the meanings of lots of words in oral language that they are not yet able to read.

Next, let's think for a moment about what you remember about learning vocabulary when you were in school. What experiences did you have? No matter how many times I ask this question to different groups of adults, responses typically include "traumatic" experiences like these:

- Each week, I had to look up a list of words in the dictionary and write out the definitions.

- I had to memorize the meanings of words using flashcards as part of test preparation.

- Each week, I had to write a sentence for each word on my vocabulary list.

A "nocturnal" animal

An animal that is awake and active at night.

We all had experiences like these, and in addition to being unpleasant, this out-of-context, drill-oriented instruction is unlikely to support text comprehension or being able to use the word in writing or speaking. We do not want to spend precious instructional time drilling primary-grade students on vocabulary, of course, but the vocabulary instruction that we all experienced (typically in older grades) may be the only way we know to teach vocabulary and why we avoid it in our K–3 classrooms.

So, before reading further, take a breath, and try to let go of whatever version of the list on the previous page was done to you as a student. We *can* support young children's vocabulary development in ways that are meaningful, motivating, engaging, and developmentally appropriate. We *can* shift the focus from memorizing word meanings for the sake of memorizing them, to supporting young children as they learn new words they can really *use*—to discuss whether or not there will be baseball practice after school; to understand, learn from, and enjoy challenging texts that they are excited to read; to be able to write about the *breathtaking scenery* on their vacation or a *courageous superhero* rather than a *fun trip* or a *good guy*.

Turn the page, and let's get started . . .

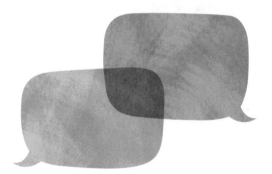

What We Know

Recent research studies that have observed instruction in large numbers of K–3 classrooms found that teachers rarely provided vocabulary instruction that was planned or cognitively challenging for their students (Carlisle, Kelcey, and Berebitsky 2013; Wright and Neuman 2014).

2

Vocabulary Development Across the Day

H Have you ever tried to read (or listen to) a text and understand it when you don't know the meanings of many of the words? Let's try it. As you read, think about what it would take for you to be able to read and comprehend this text.

If you do not know what is meant by *order-disorder duality structure, quantum theory, topological excitations, bosonic fields, fermionic, bosonization,* and *anyons,* it's hard to understand this passage. Unless you are a

We have seen in the previous chapter how the existence of an order-disorder duality structure allows the obtainment of a full quantum theory of topological excitations. In the present chapter, conversely, we will see how the same structure is at the very roots of a method by which one can generate, out of bosonic fields, new composite fields with different statistics, either fermionic or generalized. In the first case, the method is usually called bosonization and allows a full description of fermions within the bosonic theory, whereas in the second, the method provides a complete description of anyons, as the particles with generalized statistics have been called, also in the framework of the bosonic theory. (Marino 2017, 168)

physicist, you are probably unable to provide a simple explanation of these terms or the concepts they represent. And this is not only a reading challenge; it's unlikely you would be able to understand these words in conversation or use them in your own writing either. In contrast, for someone with a strong background in quantum physics, these terms likely represent important concepts they can use to comprehend this text.

None of this is your fault. None of us have grown up speaking the language of "quantum physics." Rather, these words, and the concepts that they represent, need to be learned over time in meaningful contexts, such as while studying physics.

When It Comes to Comprehension, Word Meanings *Matter*

The challenge, for all types of communication, is if we don't know what words mean, it can feel like there is a locked gate that limits comprehension. In particular, if we do not know the meaning of several vocabulary words in a text or in conversation, it is very difficult to understand the overall meaning. This is true even for highly skilled readers.

You were probably able to say the words in the physics text relatively fluently. If particular words were challenging to decode, you likely had strategies you could use to figure out how to pronounce them. You probably also have comprehension strategies you can use when you don't understand a text. For example, you know to try rereading when something is confusing and to make inferences when all of the information is not provided directly in the text. Yet, for most of us (physics majors aside), this text is *still* too challenging to read. Unfortunately, no amount of fluent decoding or strategic reading can open the locked vocabulary gate—the barrier to comprehension of this text.

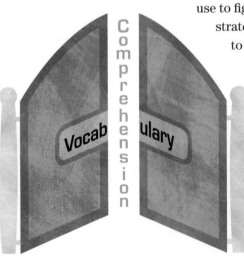

Now think about young children who are not yet highly skilled readers. Even if we spend lots of instructional time teaching decoding and strategic reading, they will continue to struggle to comprehend unless we *also* support their vocabulary development.

Even if we spend lots of instructional time teaching decoding and strategic reading, [students] will continue to struggle to comprehend text unless we also support their vocabulary development.

Vocabulary and Conceptual Knowledge Are Connected

Word

Concept

Communicate

Exchange and flow of ideas from one person to another • Ways of sharing messages, ideas, and information • Verbal, nonverbal, written • Speaking, listening, letters, notes, emails, texts, announcements, conversations, speeches, news, signals, codes, symbols, sign, transmission, dispatch, report, debate, deliberation • Computers, telephones, television, telegraph, radio • Encoding, decoding, symbols • Influenced by culture, language • Other meanings: (biology) transmit disease or transfer of information from one cell or molecule to another by chemical or electrical signal

To understand the relationship between vocabulary and knowledge, it is helpful to think of another image, an iceberg (Gotwals and Wright 2017).

When we think about vocabulary learning, we think about the word itself as only the tip of the iceberg. Children can know how to say a word without a deep understanding of the underlying concepts that the word represents. For example, a teacher might say, "One thing you can do when your feelings are hurt is communicate with your friends. Let's all say *communicate*." A child could easily repeat the word without really understanding what it means.

In contrast, children can have an initial understanding of a concept (know some of the ideas hidden on the part of the iceberg that is under the ocean) without knowing the vocabulary word to label these ideas (the visible part of the iceberg). For example, by the time they enter elementary school, children know that people have ways of sharing messages and ideas, but they may not know the term *communicate*. Other children might know the word *communicate* as well as lots of information about it, including types of communication, methods of communication, or that the word has specialized meanings when we study biology.

Think about two children who hear the following sentence during a read-aloud: "Sound can help us to communicate." One child might know many concepts associated with the word *communicate*. That child would be able to make lots of inferences to better understand the text:

> Hmmm . . . sound sometimes does help us to communicate. Like when I talk to my friends or cry when I'm hurt. But I can also communicate without sound like writing a letter or giving my friend a thumbs up. So, sound isn't the only way we communicate.

A second child who only knows that *communicate* means talk, might think:

> Yes. Sound helps me talk.

Clearly, the child with a wealth of conceptual knowledge related to the word *communicate* brings more to comprehending this text (just as the physics major brought more to the earlier text). Vocabulary and conceptual knowledge are deeply connected, and so it makes sense for children to learn new word meanings as they learn the concepts and ideas that these words represent. When we support children to learn new words in conjunction with building new ideas and knowledge, this can help to open the gate to comprehension.

What We Know

Reviews of multiple research studies show that knowledge of the meaning of words in a text and knowledge of the topic of a text both support comprehension of that text (Cervetti and Wright 2020; Stahl and Fairbanks 1986; Wright and Cervetti 2017).

What Does It Mean to Know the Meaning of a Word?

If I asked you the meaning of a word that you know really well, such as *precipitation*, you probably could not provide me with the exact dictionary definition for that word. However, you could use the word when you talk or write, and you could understand the word when someone else uses it or when you read it. For example, you could check the weather forecast and understand the information being provided. And those things are far more important for real learning and communication than being able to recite a dictionary definition.

Similarly, suppose I provided you with dictionary definitions for the words in the physics text earlier in this chapter, such as:

Anyon

An elementary particle or particle-like excitation having properties intermediate between those of bosons and fermions

Does this definition help you understand the text any better? Probably not, because it doesn't provide you with enough meaningful information or knowledge of the concepts that the word represents to be practically useful. To unlock the vocabulary gate, you would need to learn terms like this in the context of learning more about quantum physics.

When we really know the meaning of a word, when we can use that word to learn and communicate, we know far more information about it than is contained in a brief dictionary definition.

Types of Vocabulary Knowledge

An informal explanation of the word's meanings

★ *Precipitation* is water falling from the sky like rain, snow, sleet, or hail.

Synonyms or antonyms for the word

★ *Sleepy, fatigued, weary,* and *exhausted* are other ways to say *tired.*
★ *Energized, lively,* and *refreshed* are ways to say *not tired.*

Categorical information

★ An *apple* and a *papaya* are both types of fruit.

Multiple meanings of the word in different contexts

★ *Bark* is the sound made by a dog. *Bark* is also the outside covering of a woody plant.

Morphological knowledge (knowledge of the meaningful word parts inside the word)

★ The prefix *re* means again. So, *redo* means to do again, *reappear* means to appear again.

Concepts that the word represents

★ *Communication* might be verbal, nonverbal, or written.

Formal compared to slang/informal meaning of the word

★ *Cow* is an adult female of certain types of animals.
★ "Don't have a *cow!*" means don't get upset.

Slight differences between the meaning of this word and the meaning of similar words

★ *Happy* is a feeling of joy or being pleased, but *elated* is extremely happy.

Phonological knowledge

★ How to say or pronounce the word.

Orthographic knowledge

★ How to spell the word.

Discipline-specific meanings of the word

★ When we use the word *plot* while discussing literature, we likely mean the storyline or sequence of events.
★ When we talk about *plot* while discussing geography, it likely means to mark a route on a map or a piece of land.
★ When we talk about *plot* when discussing history, we likely mean a secret plan.
★ When we talk about *plot* in math or science, we likely mean a graphical technique for representing data.

Appropriate syntax for the word

★ When and how to use the word in a sentence.

As teachers, we need to understand that a formal definition, particularly when it is out of context such as on a flash card or worksheet, provides only a very limited amount of word meaning information. Formal definitions may also include other complex words, making learning word meanings even more complicated for young children (think about explaining a word that you don't understand using words that you don't understand, like in the *anyon* example earlier).

It can be helpful to think of word meaning knowledge as a continuum. We may know some but not all of the information about a word. Sometimes we hear a word and we know something about what it means, but not enough to know how to use it on our own. We use the term *receptive language* for words we can understand when someone says them or when we read them, and *expressive language* for words that we can use in speaking or writing. We often have enough knowledge about a word to understand it receptively before we feel comfortable using it expressively. In classrooms, this means that children may understand more than we know!

Light rain is called Drizzle. Thunderstorms make heavy Rain.

Writing about weather, this child shows they know the difference between *drizzle* and *heavy rain*.

A Teacher's Guide to Vocabulary Development Across the Day

In a study with sixty fourth-grade students, vocabulary depth (how well children know words) predicted reading comprehension on standardized measures. In this study, the researchers defined *depth* as students being able to provide *their own* definitions for words as well as being able to select synonyms for vocabulary words (Ouellette 2006).

How Do We Learn New Words?

We Need Repeated Exposure to Words in Meaningful Contexts

Most word knowledge is acquired incidentally, without conscious attention. We did not memorize the many thousands of word meanings we know on flashcards—we just learned them incrementally over time. As we are exposed to words that are a part of our environment (we hear them or read them), we pick up more and more precise information about their meanings.

At MY-BrthDAr PArty We HIT
MY PIYYotue AnD TIN...

A birthday party is the perfect place to learn what the word *piñata* means.

A Teacher's Guide to Vocabulary Development Across the Day

The Time I Went to the Hospital

Then they called us in.

Then they put an IV in me and my mom came in too.

Then they hooked the salt water up to the salt water bag.

It took a whole hour.

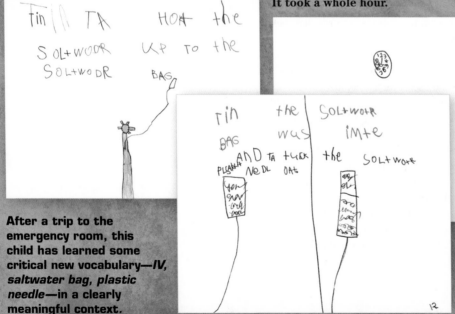

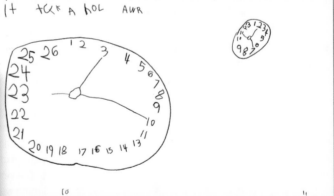

After a trip to the emergency room, this child has learned some critical new vocabulary—*IV*, *saltwater bag*, *plastic needle*—in a clearly meaningful context.

Then the salt water bag was empty and they took the salt water needle out.

Let's start at the end of this sentence—We need *repeated exposure* to words in *meaningful contexts*—and unpack the three key concepts it suggests:

Meaningful Contexts

★ When babies first learn to speak, they might overgeneralize and call all liquids *milk* or all adult males *dada*. But over time, this knowledge is refined, based on pertinent information in the environment. For example, maybe a toddler says their word for milk and receives milk but is frustrated because what they really want is water. The toddler throws the milk on the floor but keeps yelling for milk. An adult eventually offers water and uses the word *water*, thereby providing more information about both words (i.e., "It doesn't work to use the word *milk* if you want water. You need to say a different word for that.").

★ Texts, discussions, and opportunities to learn new things both in and out of school (a trip to a zoo or farm, a math lesson) can all provide meaningful contexts like this for vocabulary learning.

Exposure

★ The primary way young children (who are not yet reading independently) are exposed to new words is through adults. Adults use new words, read books that contain new words, or may provide access to media (TV shows, songs, videos) and experiences that bring new words into a child's environment. Children can also learn new words from their peers, but typically children of similar ages in similar contexts know similar words, so exposure to *new* words from peer conversation may be limited.

★ Children cannot possibly learn words that they are not exposed to. If adults use simple words ("Someone is speaking in your story; add some *talkie marks*"), those are the words children will learn and use. If we use sophisticated words ("Someone is speaking in your story; add some *quotation marks*"), children will learn and use these words. If we read to children and discuss texts, children will learn the new words that are in those texts. If we rarely read to children, they will have limited access to the vocabulary of texts. Teachers are the adults who are with children for many hours each day, so the language we expose children to in our K–3 classrooms really matters for supporting children's vocabulary development.

Repeated

★ We learn words incrementally over time, building more and more word knowledge with each exposure in a meaningful context. If we want children to learn the meanings of new words, we need to create lots of opportunities for them to hear and use the words, over time, in meaningful contexts.

We Learn Words That Are Relevant and Useful

Have you have ever traveled to a country where they speak a different language? During your trip, you probably learned words that helped you to order food or find your way, but you were less likely to learn words you didn't need to have an enjoyable trip. Children learn new words the same way—they learn what's relevant and useful. A child growing up in Michigan may learn the words for *mittens*, *scarf*, and *coat* before a child growing up in Florida.

The children who enter our classrooms have been exposed to different words based on their particular life experiences, needs, and contexts, so we can't make assumptions about what they know. If a word is important for learning something in school, we need to help children to learn it. Across the school day, we need to open the vocabulary gate so that *all* children have access to the ideas (especially those they will encounter in texts) they need for school success.

The challenge is how to teach these word meanings in ways that feel relevant and useful to young children. Learning words because they are on flashcards, worksheets, or tests will not feel relevant and useful even if the words actually are. We need an instructional approach that is more aligned with the purposeful word learning that occurs naturalistically in children's environments.

You May Be Wondering

Q: *I have used flash cards with dictionary definitions to study vocabulary and it raised my scores on my GREs. I still remember a few of the words I studied. Is there a place for this type of word study in the elementary classroom?*

A: Can people memorize definitions for a test? Absolutely. And if it is a test that requires you to know definitions then, sure, it will probably help—especially if you are motivated to do well on the test. The fact that you now remember only a few of those definitions shows that this served your purposes at the time, but that you weren't motivated to actually learn and use these words in real life to read, write, speak, listen, and learn. Memorizing definitions (for a test) is just not how we learn most words. The words that stick with us are the ones we learned in meaningful contexts such as reading, conversations, or learning new things.

A Teacher's Guide to Vocabulary Development Across the Day

We Learn Words When We Have Opportunities for Active Processing

Children are more likely to learn when they can actively engage with a word and its meaning rather than just passively receiving information from the teacher. In discussions about texts or new ideas, children have opportunities to use new words that are connected to their learning. Sometimes in these discussions, we invite children to think very specifically about a particular word or set of words that are important to learn. For example, we might:

- **Discuss images:** "What is similar about the *insects* in these pictures?"

- **Discuss objects:** "Do you know what this is? It's a *thermometer*. Can anyone tell me why we use a *thermometer*?"

- **Use movement:** "Can you stand up and show me what it looks like when someone *strolls* down the street?"

- **Think about examples:** "When is a time when you felt *exuberant*?"

- **Compare and contrast the meanings of words:** "What do you think is the difference between *giggle* and *guffaw*?"

- **Discuss multiple meanings of the same word in different contexts:** "So we know that the *seasons* are summer, winter, spring, and fall, but in this recipe it says to *season* the food. Let's talk about what that could mean."

- **Think about meaningful word parts:** "*Triangle, tricycle,* and *tripod* all have the beginning *tri*. What do we think that *tri* might mean?"

- **Think about cognates (words that exist in two different languages and have the same root or origin):** "Does the word *fantastic* sound like a word you already know in Spanish?"

- **Use new vocabulary during writing:** "What is a more precise or interesting word that you could use instead of *happy* in your writing?"

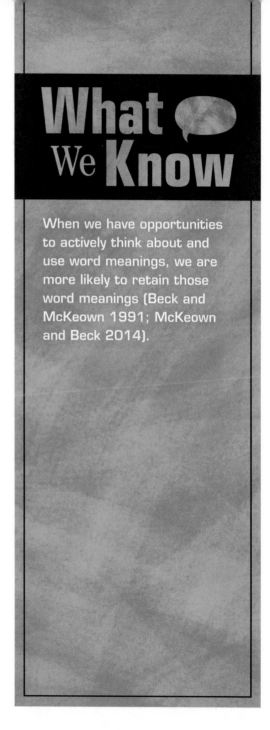

What We Know

When we have opportunities to actively think about and use word meanings, we are more likely to retain those word meanings (Beck and McKeown 1991; McKeown and Beck 2014).

We don't need to spend a long time on out-of-context vocabulary activities. Instead, we plan "brains on" opportunities for children to think about and use words in meaningful contexts during the day. When we do this, children also learn about how language works, which helps them when they encounter new words or word meanings. For example, if a familiar word is used in a new way, it is a lot less confusing if you already understand that words *can* have more than one meaning. So, when the weather report says that there is a cold *front*, we want children to know enough about language to think:

That can't mean the same thing as being in the *front* of the line at school. So, what does *front* mean here?

When Do We Learn New Words?

We Learn New Words When We Engage in Conversation

In day-to-day oral language interactions, children are exposed to words in meaningful contexts, and the words we use often when we talk with children in our classrooms are the words they will learn over time. If we regularly use sophisticated words ("Let's *observe* the weather" or "Let's *compare* these texts" or "Do you *concur* with Sara's idea?"), children will begin to understand and use these words as well. Talk is a powerful teaching tool when it comes to vocabulary development, so we need to be intentional about using new words with young children in our classrooms.

We Learn New Words When We Read

We know that vocabulary supports text comprehension—the vocabulary gate needs to be open in order to comprehend a text—but the reverse is true as well. Reading a lot is positively associated with vocabulary development. When readers comprehend a text, they can learn word meaning information for the few words they may not know in that text (Sternberg 1987). Of course, "reading a lot" for young children (who are not yet reading independently) really means that adults need to read aloud a lot. If we want to build children's vocabulary in our K–3 classrooms, we need to make time for read-alouds every single day and maybe even more than once per day.

Importantly, the language of texts is different from spoken language. In everyday conversation, the goal is typically to communicate in a clear and straightforward way, and we can use the immediate context to support our communication. For example, we might say, "Can you flip that on?" (while pointing to the light switch). Facial expressions, gestures, and the shared context help to support this clear communication.

What We Know

Studies in homes and in classrooms, beginning in the early childhood years, demonstrate that when children are exposed to explanations of sophisticated words during oral language interactions with adults in their environments, there are long-term benefits for children's vocabulary development and literacy achievement (Dickinson and Porche 2011; Weizman and Snow 2001).

In contrast, authors do not benefit from shared context, so they typically use more decontextualized language (i.e., language that is used to convey ideas that are beyond the immediate shared context). This might include discussions of worlds that are imaginary (*once upon a time . . .*) or places that are far away (*in a land far, far away*). Stories and poems may use less direct and more figurative language (metaphors, similes, allusions) because the goal is to help the reader feel a character's emotions or visualize a scene. Authors of informational text may discuss categories (Why are spiders not considered *insects*?) or concepts (What is a *community*?). Because of this specialized language, texts include vocabulary that we rarely use in everyday speech and provide lots of opportunities to expose children to new words. The more children experience and learn the *vocabulary of text*, the easier it is for them to comprehend new texts.

We Learn New Words When We Learn New Things

Every topic, domain, or area of knowledge has associated vocabulary. There are words associated with science, social studies, and math, but also with different sports or the arts. My children participate in theater, and along with many other new "theater" words I've had to learn (*sitzprobe, vomitory*), I recently learned that the edges of the stage are called the *legs* of the stage. Beyond the legs, the actor cannot be seen by the audience. (Some people think that the reason we wish actors good luck by saying "break a leg" is because we hope they make it past the "legs" and onto the actual stage.) Understanding this familiar word in a totally new context opens new ideas and possibilities.

This young writer demonstrates knowledge of the concepts of *echo* by repeating the word *eaten* and making the letters get smaller with each repitition.

> Chapter 2 the cave.
>
> Name cruz   Date
>
> Phew. Said Chase. Those wolfs are gone. I'm not going to be eatn. eatn. eatn eatn. The cave echos. Said Chase.

Think about your own experiences of learning new things that may not have been part of formal schooling. If you decide to start running marathons, you would probably learn and use terms like *cadence* and *foot strike* or ~~specialized running~~-related meanings for words like *splits* or *form*. If you decide to take up ~~gardening~~, you would need to learn plant names (*hydrangea*), plant parts (*pistil*), ~~plant types~~ (*perennials*), the words for the tools to use (*trowel, shears*), the words for the work you would do (*pruning, deadheading*), including special gardening meanings for everyday words (a *cutting* or an *annual*).

All this applies to school as well. In order to create opportunities for young children to learn new words, we need to build their knowledge of the world and make sure that they are learning new things. They need lots of time to engage in content-area learning, including science, social studies, math, the arts, and physical education.

As Aiden learned about whale sharks, he learned topic-related vocabulary such as *plankton* and *endangered*: I use my mouth to swallow small fish and plankton and other small things. Whale sharks are endangered.

You May Be Wondering

Q : *Which words should children learn?*

A : Whenever I am asked this question, I usually joke that the answer is: all of them! I say this because if a child does not know the meaning of a word, it never hurts to learn it. And, of course, we always want children to understand the texts, conversations, and learning that happen in school, and this includes knowing the word meanings that will help them to understand and participate. So, if a word comes up that a child doesn't know, it is always a good idea to open the vocabulary gate and discuss its meaning.

The challenge with vocabulary is that there are so many words to learn in our language. Some researchers (e.g., Paris 2005) have referred to vocabulary as an "unconstrained" skill, meaning that the number of words to learn is almost unlimited, compared to "constrained skills" such as alphabet knowledge, where there are just twenty-six letters for children to know. But the challenge is also an exciting opportunity, because there are so many wonderful words for children to learn. That said, instructional time is precious and we do need to think about which words we'll select to support children's vocabulary development, so we'll revisit this question again in the pages that follow.

In order to create opportunities
for young children to learn
new words, we need to build
their knowledge of the world
and make sure that they are
learning new things.

Why Should We Think Differently About Vocabulary Instruction?

Recent studies of vocabulary instruction in the early years of school have shown that a year of schooling is unlikely to impact children's vocabulary learning trajectory at all (Christian et al. 2000; Skibbe et al. 2011)! This finding made me wonder how this could possibly be, so my colleague Susan Neuman and I followed up with several studies of curriculum and instruction including observing for 660 hours in fifty-five kindergarten classrooms as well as studying the most commonly used English language arts (ELA) core curriculum materials (Wright and Neuman 2013, 2014). Here is what we found:

Teachers rarely provided planned vocabulary instruction. They typically explained word meanings to children when they thought children did not understand, but they only explained words once, in the teachable moment. This meant that children had only one exposure to new words and no opportunities at all to use or apply these words. While this probably helped children to comprehend the text or learning in the moment, children would be unlikely to retain very much information about these words from this type of instruction.

Teachers were more likely to explain word meanings to children in teachable moments when they taught more affluent student populations. Teachers were least likely to explain words when they taught in schools where more than 50 percent of children received free and reduced lunch. So, even teachable moment vocabulary supports were inequitably distributed from classroom to classroom.

When teachers used a core reading curriculum, this made no difference at all to the teachable-moments-only vocabulary instruction that we observed. This was surprising, so we examined core curriculum materials to try to understand their supports for vocabulary instruction. We found that these materials provided teachers with a list of vocabulary to teach each week (although the number of words ranged greatly across curricula from two to twenty), a definition, and an example sentence to use when introducing the word meaning to children. But, they rarely supported teachers in doing more than introducing word meanings. Also, it was not always clear how the selected words related to ongoing learning in the classroom.

What we learned from these studies is that if we want to support children's vocabulary development, we are going to need to do something very different. We cannot teach one word per day or five words per week or only explain word meanings coincidentally when they come up. If we want to make a difference, we have to be intentional and make plans to support children to learn word meanings across all parts of the school day.

Take a Moment to Reflect

In the sections that follow, we'll dig into the practical application of all you've read about so far, but before we do, take a moment to think about these questions:

Can you think of moments when you were surprised by your students' word knowledge?

Can you think of times when vocabulary in a book or in oral language caused confusion for students in your classroom?

How do you support children's vocabulary instruction in your classroom now? How does this align with what you have learned in this chapter about vocabulary development?

Learn More

Neuman, S. B., and T. S. Wright. 2014. "The Magic of Words: Teaching Vocabulary in the Early Childhood Classroom." *American Educator*, 38(2): 4–13. www.aft.org /periodical/american -educator/summer-2014 /magic-words.

Cobb, Charlene, and Camille Blachowicz. 2014. *No More "Look Up the List" Vocabulary Instruction*. Portsmouth, NH: Heinemann.

Vocabulary Development During Read-Alouds

For most teachers and children, reading and enjoying a book together is a favorite part of the school day. Read-alouds also provide a meaningful and important context for vocabulary learning. I still remember sitting in an elementary classroom listening to my teacher read *Charlotte's Web*. I learned the word *salutations* when Charlotte first greets Wilbur in the barn, and *humble* when Charlotte writes this last word in her web before she dies. Books bring wonderful new words into our classrooms and into children's lives.

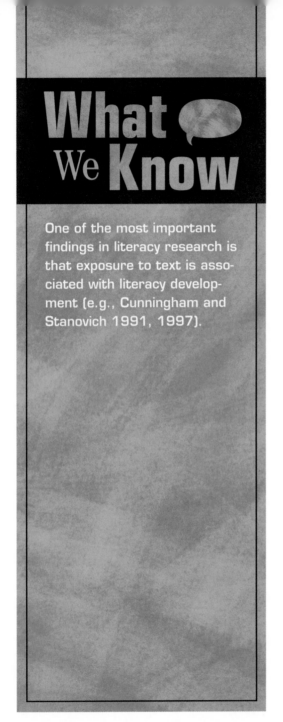

What We Know

One of the most important findings in literacy research is that exposure to text is associated with literacy development (e.g., Cunningham and Stanovich 1991, 1997).

We know that children cannot learn new vocabulary unless they are exposed to the words in their environment, and reading aloud is one way to bring new words into a child's environment. Texts open up worlds of possibilities for language development and use that would not otherwise exist inside the walls of a classroom. Through books, we can travel to new places—real or imaginary. Think about the way that Ezra Jack Keats transports you to a snowy day in the city, or Maurice Sendak takes you to where the wild things are.

Through books, we can visit different time periods, we can gather information to understand new ideas, we can learn about other people's experiences, and we can feel emotions that move beyond our day-to-day lives. And we do all of this *with words*.

salutations

A salutation is a greeting. For example, if you say hello to someone or write "Dear" and the person's name at the start of a letter, those are salutations.

Read-alouds are particularly important in the early grades because children experience words and concepts that they cannot yet access independently as readers. Even without any instruction at all, words and ideas can be learned incidentally, just from engaging with a wide variety of texts during read-alouds. To maximize the impact of this learning, however, we make plans to support children's vocabulary development as we read aloud, remembering what does and doesn't work.

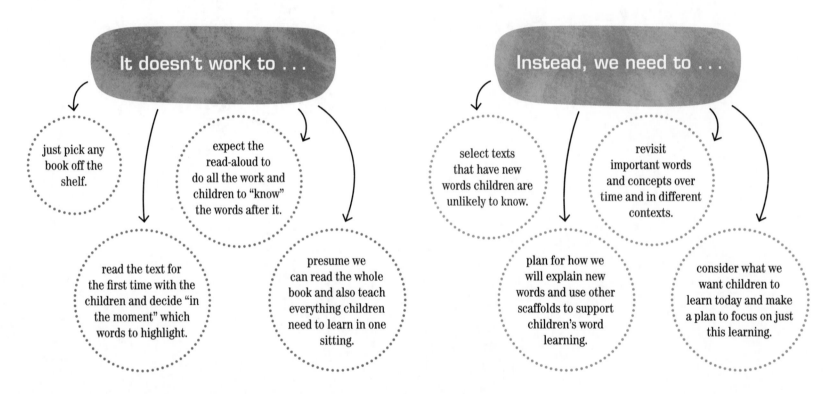

It doesn't work to . . .

just pick any book off the shelf.

expect the read-aloud to do all the work and children to "know" the words after it.

read the text for the first time with the children and decide "in the moment" which words to highlight.

presume we can read the whole book and also teach everything children need to learn in one sitting.

Instead, we need to . . .

select texts that have new words children are unlikely to know.

revisit important words and concepts over time and in different contexts.

plan for how we will explain new words and use other scaffolds to support children's word learning.

consider what we want children to learn today and make a plan to focus on just this learning.

The key is, we need to be *intentional* about text selection, about explaining words before or during reading, and about revisiting important or conceptually challenging words after reading the text.

The key is, we need to be *intentional* about text selection, about explaining words before or during reading, and about revisiting important or conceptually challenging words after reading the text.

Select Texts Thoughtfully

It may seem obvious, but for children to learn new words when we read aloud to them, we need to read texts that include words children are unlikely to know. In the early grades, this typically means trade books that children cannot yet read and comprehend independently. Read-alouds are a great time to encounter new vocabulary because the teacher is there to help, to explain, and to clarify—to open the vocabulary gate for children.

Of course, many of the books in primary classrooms are written for "early readers" and they typically have *controlled* vocabulary, words that young children are already likely to know. Designed to keep the vocabulary gate wide open, these books support independent reading because when children can decode a word accurately, they can easily connect it to a meaning that they already know. But texts for beginning readers are unlikely to support children in developing *new* vocabulary knowledge, so they're not good choices for a read-aloud if vocabulary learning is the goal.

Both kinds of texts are important. Children need opportunities to build new vocabulary during read-alouds at the same time that they are learning to read independently. Why? Because as their reading skill develops, the texts children are expected to read will become *less* controlled and they will need more and more vocabulary knowledge to support their comprehension of the challenging new words and ideas in more advanced texts.

What We Know

Research shows that *extra-textual talk* (i.e., the talk that happens around the text) facilitates children's literacy development in the elementary grades (Greene Brabham and Lynch-Brown 2002; Varelas and Pappas 2006). These studies demonstrate that children learn more vocabulary and have stronger text comprehension when they have opportunities to discuss words and ideas in a text.

One study demonstrated that when the teacher provided brief word explanations during reading, children learned meanings for about 22 percent of new vocabulary just from that brief, one-time explanation (Biemiller and Boote 2006). So, in addition to supporting comprehension, explaining word meanings during reading can give children a small vocabulary learning boost as well.

Plan Ahead for Teaching

Explain Word Meanings in Context

One way to support children's comprehension of a read-aloud text is to explain word meanings *during* the read-aloud. After reading a line of text with a difficult vocabulary word that children may not know, we can stop and briefly discuss or explain the meaning of the word—opening the vocabulary gate that can limit comprehension.

When we explain new or challenging words, it's important that our explanations are *child-friendly* and that we use language or images that are already familiar to children (Beck, McKeown, and Kucan 2013). Let's look at a few examples on the next page.

Examples of Child-Friendly Explanations

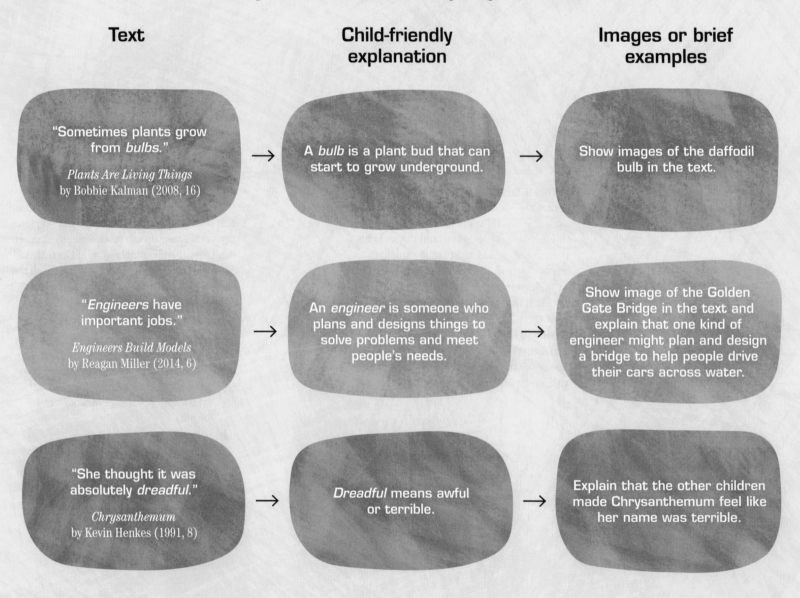

Text	Child-friendly explanation	Images or brief examples
"Sometimes plants grow from *bulbs*." *Plants Are Living Things* by Bobbie Kalman (2008, 16)	A *bulb* is a plant bud that can start to grow underground.	Show images of the daffodil bulb in the text.
"*Engineers* have important jobs." *Engineers Build Models* by Reagan Miller (2014, 6)	An *engineer* is someone who plans and designs things to solve problems and meet people's needs.	Show image of the Golden Gate Bridge in the text and explain that one kind of engineer might plan and design a bridge to help people drive their cars across water.
"She thought it was absolutely *dreadful*." *Chrysanthemum* by Kevin Henkes (1991, 8)	*Dreadful* means awful or terrible.	Explain that the other children made Chrysanthemum feel like her name was terrible.

Child-Friendly Explanations . . .

are a good idea whenever children might not know a word meaning *and* when understanding the meaning is important for comprehending the text.

★ There are no right or wrong words to explain during read-alouds and no certain number to aim for. If you think children—or even a few children—may not understand the meaning of a word, go ahead and plan to explain it briefly—especially if the word is important for understanding the overall meaning of the text. This won't hurt children who already know the word, and the explanation can be enormously helpful for children who don't. Explaining word meanings in context opens the vocabulary gate so all children can engage with, enjoy, and learn from read-aloud texts.

are brief and tied directly to the context of the text.

★ The purpose of a child-friendly explanation is to help children better understand the current text they are reading. Make sure your explanations don't take up too much time, so children don't lose the meaningful flow of the text, and make sure that the explanation focuses on the meaning of the word in this *particular* text. Think like a Lemony Snicket or Fancy Nancy book. These texts actually provide child-friendly explanations that are directly tied to the context of the text:

   ★ In Jane O'Connor's *Fancy Nancy: Poison Ivy Expert*, the text says: "We conceal everything. (Conceal is a fancy word for hid)."

   ★ In Lemony Snicket's *The Reptile Room: Or, Murder!*, the text says: " 'It's a misnomer,' he said, using a word which here means 'a very wrong name.' "

Unfortunately, it is rare to find this information provided in texts, so in most cases, teachers have to do this work.

use language, images, or motions that children already know.

★ The goal of a child-friendly explanation is to support comprehension, so be sure not to use other complicated words in your explanation. Use clear, simple language and, if it makes sense, clear images (in the text or to supplement the text) or motions. You could also use a combination of these. For example, to explain the word *stride*, you could say "a long step" and then stand up and briefly show the children how you stride across the classroom. Then, continue reading.

are planned before the read-aloud.

★ It can be very challenging to come up with a brief and clear child-friendly explanation without taking time to think about it, so it's important to plan ahead. In most cases, when you read the text ahead of time, you can make a pretty good guess at which words might get in the way of comprehension for children in your class. Of course, anything can happen, and children may look confused or ask the meaning of a word you thought they knew. In this case, do your best, and then remember to plan an explanation of the word for the next time you read the text with a class.

are supportive for bilingual students.

★ Explanations that use images, actions, or words children already know help bilingual children to learn new vocabulary and to access and comprehend texts in English. Before reading aloud, consider which words bilingual children may not know in English (and which are important to comprehending the text) so you'll be ready with explanations. And remember, as long as you are artfully brief and clear, it does no harm for all children to hear words explained in context—even if they already know them. In fact, hearing a word meaning in the *particular* context of a text may deepen children's conceptual knowledge (under the iceberg) of the word.

Types of Challenging Words

Let's take a moment to think about the types of words that are likely to be challenging in literature and informational texts.

Which types of words are important to explain?

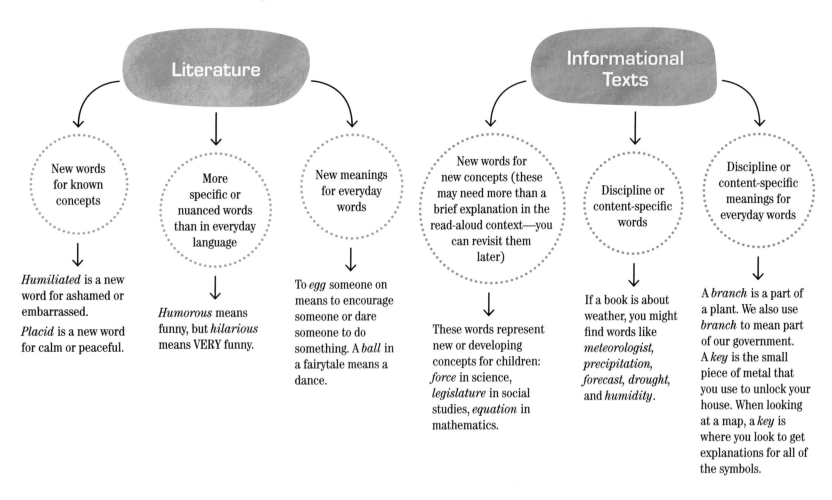

Literature

New words for known concepts

↓

Humiliated is a new word for ashamed or embarrassed.

Placid is a new word for calm or peaceful.

More specific or nuanced words than in everyday language

↓

Humorous means funny, but *hilarious* means VERY funny.

New meanings for everyday words

↓

To *egg* someone on means to encourage someone or dare someone to do something. A *ball* in a fairytale means a dance.

Informational Texts

New words for new concepts (these may need more than a brief explanation in the read-aloud context—you can revisit them later)

↓

These words represent new or developing concepts for children: *force* in science, *legislature* in social studies, *equation* in mathematics.

Discipline or content-specific words

↓

If a book is about weather, you might find words like *meteorologist, precipitation, forecast, drought,* and *humidity*.

Discipline or content-specific meanings for everyday words

↓

A *branch* is a part of a plant. We also use *branch* to mean part of our government. A *key* is the small piece of metal that you use to unlock your house. When looking at a map, a *key* is where you look to get explanations for all of the symbols.

To prepare for the read-aloud, write the selected word, the page number where it occurs in the text, and the child-friendly explanation you've planned on a sticky note (one for each word). Place the notes on the outside back cover of the text where you can see them as you read. If the child-friendly explanations work well (i.e., children seem to understand the text where the word is used), consider transferring the explanation to permanent labels inside the back cover so you can use them again.

A teacher's notes to guide her child-friendly explanations for *Hello, Autumn!* **by Shelley Rotner**

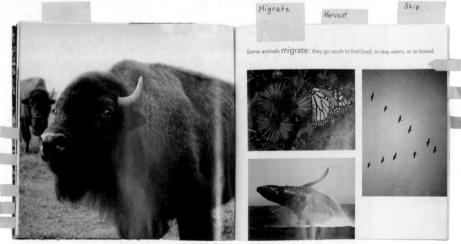

For help with planning child-friendly explanations, check out resources such as wordsmyth .net, which is an online dictionary for kids. This website explains words using language that children are likely to understand. I often start with this type of resource and then adjust to make sure that I think the children I am reading with will understand all of the words in the explanation.

▶ Video 3.1

Teachers offer child-friendly explanations of vocabulary in context.

You Try It

Take a look at these three text excerpts. Which words would you select for brief, child-friendly explanations? How would you explain the words that you have selected to children in your class?

Families by Shelley Rotner and Sheila Kelly

"When members of a family live far away, they like to visit. They get together at celebrations and reunions."

How Do Plants Survive? by Kelley MacAulay

"Plants cannot move around to find food or water. They must survive in the place where they are growing."

Dear Juno by Soyung Pak

"And he wondered if any of the planes came from a little town near Seoul where his grandmother lived, and where she ate persimmons every evening before bed."

Remember that a child-friendly explanation provides just enough information to help children to understand the read-aloud text. If we want children to learn new vocabulary well enough to understand it *and* use it for their own learning, we need to provide additional meaningful opportunities for children to interact with the new word—both before reading and after reading.

Writing is a great way for children to use new words and concepts, such as the term *life cycle* when writing about bears.

Explore Words Before and After Reading

Not all words work well for brief child-friendly explanations *during* the read-aloud. For example, it's hard to define words that represent new and challenging concepts (e.g., *photosynthesis, molecule, shadow, opportunity cost, trade, quadrilateral*) in a brief way that helps children understand the text. Remember how the definition of *anyon* didn't really help us comprehend the physics text earlier? Children learn these kinds of words best when they have opportunities to build rich conceptual knowledge, so it's a good idea to plan for more in-depth learning around them before and after reading the text in order to open the vocabulary gate for children.

Let's consider an example. In the text *Geoffrey Groundhog Predicts the Weather*, by Bruce Koscielniak, some words are easy to explain using child-friendly explanations in context. When discussing the title, for instance, we could explain that "*predicts* means to tell ahead of time that something will happen. So, Geoffrey can tell ahead of time what the weather will be." Or in the sentence, "One morning, after a long winter's nap, Geoffrey Groundhog popped out of his burrow to look for his shadow," we could explain that *burrow* means "a hole or tunnel dug by certain animals for use as a hiding place or home. So Geoffrey Groundhog's burrow is his home under the ground."

In contrast, the concept of *shadows* and how they work is much more challenging. In the plot of this text, Geoffrey has difficulty seeing his shadow because of the many lights and flashes caused by the news and TV cameras. Without some understanding of how shadows are formed, the problem in this text makes little sense. If we want children to comprehend the plot, a broader exploration of the concept of shadows seems necessary (perhaps time to explore with light sources and various objects to understand how shadows work) both *before* reading the text and then to deepen knowledge *after* reading.

Previewing the word *autumn* on a seasons wheel before the read-aloud

A Teacher's Guide to Vocabulary Development Across the Day

Explicit Instruction: Understanding Words More Deeply

Sometimes, we want to make sure that children learn particular words. They might be conceptually rich words (like *shadow*), words that will be useful for learning content, or words that are likely to occur regularly in other texts. They may also be words that we want children to learn so they can incorporate more precise language into their writing.

When we want children to learn specific words, we apply the principles of word learning and plan for brief and focused interactions with these words after the read-aloud (we can always revisit the text later if we want to explore more or if the concept is more complex). Let's revisit those principles now and imagine them at work with the word *shadow*.

We Need Lots of Word Meaning Information

- Have children say the word: "Can you say *shadow*?"

- Show children the spelling of the word: "This is the word *shadow* [write on chart paper]. The *S* and *H* together make the /sh/ sound. The *A* makes the /a/ sound. The *D* makes the /d/ sound. And, the *O* and *W* work together to make the /oh/ sound."

- Depending on the word, use movement, physical objects, photographs, images, or video to support meaning. Have children use flashlights and their fingers to make shadows: "What happens if two or three flashlights are shined on your fingers from different directions? Can you still see a shadow? How is this like what happened to Geoffrey in the book?"

- Discuss multiple meanings of the word: "What would it mean if I say, 'Sarah, since it is your first day of school, can you shadow Aliyah today?'"

- If appropriate, discuss category membership. For example, an *X* is a type of *Y*.

- If appropriate, discuss meaningful word parts.

What We Know

Studies of vocabulary development with young children demonstrate that children learn the most vocabulary when teachers include both implicit (i.e., using sophisticated vocabulary with children, lots of read-alouds with child-friendly explanations) and explicit (teaching particular words) vocabulary instruction (Marulis and Neuman 2010).

We Need Exposure in Meaningful Contexts

- Revisit the page or pages in the book where the word is used: "So, we've figured out that a shadow is a dark area that is made when something opaque blocks the light. Let's look back at the page where Geoffrey has trouble seeing because of all the people crowding around and the camera lights flashing. Why do you think Geoffrey can't see his shadow in this situation?"

We Learn Words That Are Relevant and Useful

- Discuss examples of how the word is used in contexts that are relevant to children's lives: "Have you ever seen a shadow in our classroom? Where? Let's go outside and see if we can find any shadows on the playground."

- Encourage children to use the new word in discussion: "What did you notice about shadows when we looked for shadows on the playground?"

- Connect words to children's personal experiences: "Have you ever noticed your own shadow? What did you notice?"

We Learn Words When We Have Opportunities for Active Processing

- Compare and contrast word meanings. Compare *opaque* and *translucent* objects. Use a flashlight to help children figure out which ones make shadows.

- Ask children to use new words in text-based discussions.

- Read an informational book about shadows, such as *Light: Shadows, Mirrors, and Rainbows,* by Natalie Rosinsky. See what you can learn that helps you to understand Geoffrey's problem.

- Ask children to use new words in their writing: "Let's draw a picture of a shadow that we find on the playground. Can you write about what you see?"

▶ Video 3.2

Revisiting important vocabulary after the read-aloud.

A Teacher's Guide to Vocabulary Development Across the Day

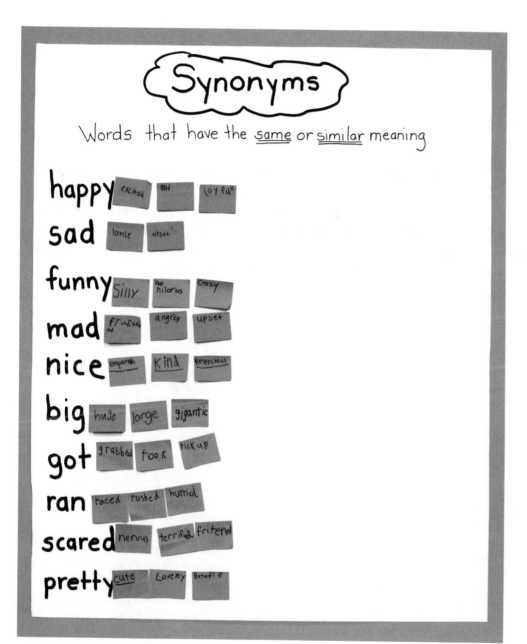

Synonyms

Words that have the <u>same</u> or <u>similar</u> meaning

happy — excited, glad, ioyfull

sad — lonle, upset

funny — silly, <u>ho</u> hilarius, crazy

mad — frustrad, angrey, upset

nice — empathic, <u>kind</u>, respectful

big — huge, large, gigantic

got — grabbed, took, pickup

ran — raced, rushed, hurried

scared — nervus, terrified, fritened

pretty — <u>cute</u>, <u>lovely</u>, Betafle

A class chart of synonyms

Tip!

Early in the school year, read *The Word Collector*, by Peter H. Reynolds, and then begin some class word collections. As you find wonderful new words in read-alouds, use a wall chart, binder, or digital storage system that children can access easily and independently, and collect and group words with similar meanings. For example, when you find the new word *exuberant* during a read-aloud, add it to your Happy Words collection. When you find the word *saunter*, add it to your Walking Words collection. Encourage children to become word collectors at home and in their independent reading as well, and to add words they find to these class lists. Then, encourage children to consult the lists, particularly when they are writing: "I see that you wrote 'I had fun' and I'm wondering if you can use our Word Collections binder to find a more specific word for *fun* so that your readers know exactly how you felt?"

Text-Based Discussions: Using Words to Make Meaning

In the spring, a second-grade class is focusing on characters and character traits in their reading, and they have been learning new vocabulary words to help them as they discuss—words like *resilient, flexible, confident, clever,* and *sympathetic* are on an anchor chart on the wall.

Before reading *Cinderella,* by Marcia Brown, their teacher asks the children to think about the following open-ended questions: "Do you think Cinderella is a strong or weak character? Can you share evidence for your ideas?" After reading, the children first turn and talk to a friend, and then they share their ideas with the whole class. Notice how they are using the new vocabulary they have learned (from their study and from the text itself) in an authentic and meaningful context as they discuss the text.

ROBERT: Cinderella is *clever.* That makes you a strong character. She tricked her sisters into thinking that she isn't going to the ball.

CASSIE: I agree with Robert. She is *resilient* because when it doesn't go her way, she just tries again.

OMAR: Also, when it doesn't go her way, she is *flexible.* She is *flexible* when she couldn't go to the ball. She is *confident* that the slipper will fit her. That's our evidence from the book so you believe me. So, that's my proof from the book, yeah, that she's a strong character.

SKYLYN: She wasn't *confident* when she didn't think she would get to go the ball. If she was strong, she would speak up for herself. A weak character means not really standing up for yourself and just listening and not doing what you want. So, I think she's more like a weak character.

When children talk about a read-aloud, they are likely to use and refer to the language of the text, but the focus is not on the meaning of individual words. In discussions, we are interested in how words work together to convey meaning and whether children can explain and apply broader ideas in the text. A rich discussion after reading is the perfect way to make words feel relevant and useful. Here are some ideas to help you plan for more extended and open-ended discussions after a read-aloud:

Describe and discuss graphics (e.g., photos, illustrations, diagrams).

Ask children to think about how their own experiences and knowledge can help them to understand the text more deeply or fill in gaps where something is not stated directly. If the author writes, "the clouds turned a dark shade of gray," we want children to think, *maybe a storm is coming or maybe something bad is about to happen.*

Ask children to find evidence from the book to answer an open-ended question: "Can you share some evidence from the book? What did you read that helps you know that?"

Discuss authors' language choices: "What do you think the author means by 'sound falls round me like rain on other folks'?" (*I Live in Music* by Ntozake Shange). "Let's discuss why the subtitle of this book is 'an unexpected diversion.' What could that mean?" (*Knuffle Bunny Free: An Unexpected Diversion* by Mo Willems).

Ask children to discuss their ideas and plan their contributions with a partner or in a small group before sharing them with the whole class. This is particularly helpful for children who may be reticent in large group discussions.

Use sentence starters: "The most surprising thing I learned in this text is _____."

"Why do you think the author said _____?"

Ask open-ended questions (that suggest more than one answer):

"Do you think _____ could really happen? Why or why not?"

"What did the author want us to learn?"

"Do you agree that _____? Why or why not?"

"How does this add to what we already understand from (another text or another learning experience)?"

Act out stories. Use props, puppets, costumes. Make it fun!

Revisit interesting pages (in informational texts) or important plot points (in literature).

Ask children to "add on" to what another child says: "Can anyone add on to what Liam just said?"

Find Time to Read Aloud Often

We know that read-alouds are critical for children's literacy development and particularly for supporting vocabulary and knowledge building beyond what children may experience in their everyday lives.

An important first step for supporting children's vocabulary development, then, is to make time to read aloud *at least* once per day in K–3 classrooms. This can be challenging when there are so many competing goals and limited instructional time, so here are some possibilities for making more time to read aloud.

Read only part of the text.

★ There is no rule that you need to read an entire text in one sitting. It is okay to read part of a story one day and then pick up where you left off the following day. Just make sure to help children remember what has happened so far. For informational text, it is fine to use the table of contents and read only the parts of the text that answer specific questions or align with content-area learning goals.

Reread a text for different purposes.

★ Sometimes teachers feel like they have to do a "kitchen sink" read-aloud where—in addition to reading the text—they review the terms *author* and *illustrator*, teach five vocabulary words, review a comprehension strategy, ask children to do a retell, and then do an extension activity related to the text. Suddenly, the read-aloud has taken an hour of the school day, and children are restless, distracted, and disengaged. If you find a wonderful text with opportunities for supporting many learning goals, consider selecting one or two purposes for a particular reading and then revisiting the text at a different time with different purposes or goals in mind.

Include read-alouds across content areas.

★ Sometimes we think of read-alouds as only appropriate during times of the day designated for ELA or "reading" instruction. But read-alouds can and should happen across subject areas during the school day. Books support and enhance content-area learning by exposing children to words and concepts beyond what they might experience in firsthand investigations. For example, a child in the Midwest can learn words and concepts about the ocean, or a child in the twenty-first century can learn words and concepts about life before modern transportation.

What We Know

In the study described earlier that included 660 hours of classroom observations, we found that on average kindergarten teachers spent only 8.36 minutes per day on read-alouds of fiction and 1.7 minutes per day on read-alouds of informational text (Wright 2014). Because these are averages, these findings tell us that in some classrooms, we saw no read-alouds at all, and in many classrooms, there were no read-alouds of informational text.

Encourage Families to Read Aloud

If children experience read-alouds at school and at home, it doubles their opportunities to learn new words and ideas. And even though families are busy, and it can be hard to find time to read aloud, many caregivers want to learn more about how they can best support their young readers at home.

Here are some ways you can encourage and support families to read aloud with their children:

Explain *why* adults should continue to read aloud.

★ Often, families mistakenly believe that once children begin to read independently, then reading is no longer necessary or encouraged. They think their job should shift to supporting only the child's independent reading. But for readers to grow, they have to keep learning new words and developing new knowledge, and read-alouds expose children to more sophisticated vocabulary and content than they can access independently (while they are learning to decode).

Help families access books through community resources.

★ Consider library field trips where you help children to get their own library cards. Share information with families about community resources for book finding, or host events that collect and redistribute used books.

Send read-aloud books home.

★ We often send home books for children to practice reading independently and fluently. But if we want families to read texts that will support children's vocabulary development, we also need to send home books that are specifically designated for adults to read aloud *with* children. These books should be filled with challenging vocabulary and interesting ideas that children don't already know. If you have a lending library, consider having children select two kinds of books to take home—some to read on their own and some for a family member or friend to read aloud. This includes books for summer reading as well.

Make read-aloud book recommendations.

★ Include these in newsletters or display them where families will see them when they are in the classroom.

Tip!

To get started, look carefully at your schedule and find ten to fifteen minutes (any time during the day) for a vocabulary-focused interactive read-aloud.

1. Select a text with words your students may not know.

2. Plan child-friendly explanations and write them on sticky notes to put in the book.

3. Plan opportunities for active processing after the read-aloud—questions for discussion, pictures, movement, drama, etc. Be creative and have fun!

Offer tips on how to read aloud.

★ Remind families that—just like in school—the most important way to support children's learning when they read aloud is to explain challenging words and discuss the meaning of the texts they are reading. Consider sending home lists of prompts, questions, or suggestions for families to use when they talk with their children about the texts they share.

Encourage families to read aloud in their home language.

★ For bilingual families, consider sending home books in the child's home language. Learning words and ideas is important across languages to support children's bilingualism and biliteracy. Recently, publishers have been releasing more and more dual-language books like Pat Mora's *Water Rolls, Water Rises / El agua rueda, el agua sube* (2014). Sending a book like this home lets families choose to read together in the language that is most comfortable and enjoyable for them.

Learn More

Wright, T.S. 2019. "Reading to Learn from the Start: The Power of Interactive Read-Alouds." *American Educator* 42(4). www.aft.org/ae /winter2018-2019/wright.

If children experience read-alouds at school and at home, it doubles their opportunities to learn new words and ideas.

4

Vocabulary Development
During
Content-Area
Learning

Because of our shared history in schools, lots of people think of "vocabulary" as if it were its own content area, where you learn words just for the sake of learning them. But we know that random word learning just doesn't stick. Instead, when we remember that *we learn new words when we learn new things*, we open up so many opportunities to support children to learn vocabulary across the day. Words represent important new concepts and ideas in math, science and engineering, the social studies, and the arts, and in the specific disciplines that we teach within these content areas (e.g., civics within social studies, or physics within science). And when words are tied to concepts children are learning and experiences they are having, children are much more likely to remember them. Let's think about *why* that is, and then we'll consider *how* to do the teaching that promotes word learning in content areas.

During science we compared umbrellas with trees. We learned that umbrellas fly away easily, but trees don't. The wind catches the umbrella and forces it up. Wind goes through the leaves and branches. Umbrellas don't have roots, but trees do. Umbrellas are rigid, but trees can bend.

This chart shows how children are learning new words that help them think about what happens to trees compared to umbrellas when there is wind.

Why Teach Vocabulary *with* New Content? Because . . .

Knowledge Supports Reading Comprehension

There is value, of course, in children learning about content simply to engage with that content—in other words, to learn about science so they can know about science. But knowledge is also critical for supporting reading comprehension.

In a review of a large number of studies, my colleague and I have found overwhelming evidence that knowledge related to the *content* of a text supports comprehension of that text (Cervetti and Wright 2020). In one classic study, researchers asked "high ability" and "low ability" (their terms) readers to read a text about baseball. Some of the readers in each group had a lot of knowledge about baseball; others had very little. The authors found that knowledge supported reading comprehension, even for the "low ability" readers. In other words, having a lot of knowledge of the topic of a text may actually compensate for lower reading skills (Recht and Leslie 1988).

Children build knowledge through experiences (e.g., a trip to the pumpkin farm, a family reunion or celebration, playing a sport, visiting a new city), through reading, through conversations, and of course, through content-area instruction in school. The challenge is that multiple studies (and anecdotal evidence) suggest that schools rarely make time for content-area learning in the early grades of school. We seem to believe that the need to get kids reading and writing and doing basic math leaves little time for science, social studies, or the arts. Ironically, this contradicts everything we know about the importance of knowledge and vocabulary for text comprehension. In fact, a critical first step to supporting vocabulary development is to engage children in *regular* opportunities for content-area learning.

What We Know

In our study in fifty-five kindergarten classrooms (described earlier), we found that teachers were most likely to explain word meanings to children during read-alouds, science, and social studies.

Unfortunately, on average, teachers spent very little time on science (2.3 minutes per day), social studies (1.19 minutes per day), or read-alouds of informational texts (1.37 minutes per day). Because these numbers are averages, what they really mean is that teachers rarely provided science, social studies, or informational text read-alouds, all of which are essential opportunities for children to build knowledge and vocabulary!

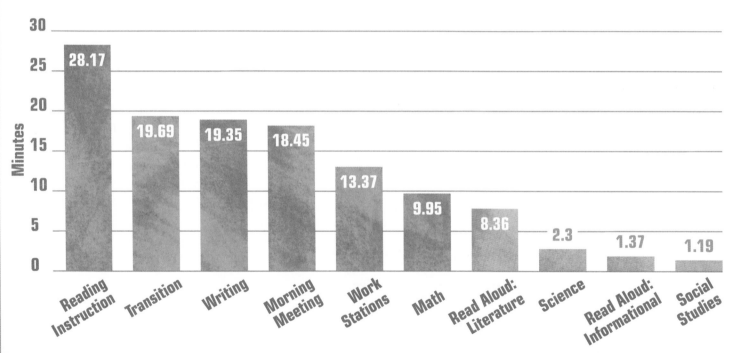

Instructional Time

Category	Minutes
Reading Instruction	28.17
Transition	19.69
Writing	19.35
Morning Meeting	18.45
Work Stations	13.37
Math	9.95
Read Aloud: Literature	8.36
Science	2.3
Read Aloud: Informational	1.37
Social Studies	1.19

Average Time Spent in Content-Area Instruction • Wright and Neuman (2014)

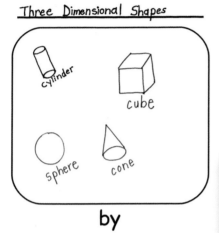

All About

Three Dimensional Shapes

cylinder

cube

sphere

cone

by

Ms. Smith's Class

A kindergarten teacher uses the discipline-specific word *vertices* in interactive writing as her students learn about different shapes.

Discipline-Specific Language Is Different from Everyday Language

The discipline-specific language that children need to learn academic content often includes entirely different words from those we use in everyday conversations. We rarely spend time at home discussing *equations*, *seed dispersal*, a *color wheel* or an *archipelago*. Children learn about *equations* as they study math, *seed dispersal* as they study science, *color wheels* as they learn about art, and *archipelagos* when they look at maps in social studies or study land formations in science. As a high school physics teacher I once knew said, "No one grows up speaking physics at home."

So when we teach new content, we also teach children the words they need to talk about their developing knowledge and understandings. We cannot expect children to show up at school already knowing the language of particular disciplines, and we cannot think of vocabulary as something that children learn *only* during ELA. Typically, ELA curricula do not even consider the words that children will need to support their learning and communicating in other content areas. The bottom line is that we need to think about word learning as part of (rather than separate from) all content area learning.

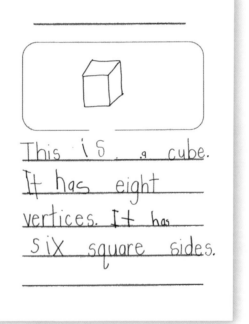

This is a cube.
It has eight
vertices. It has
six square sides.

Common Words Often Have Discipline-Specific Meanings

Many common words have different, specific meanings in particular content areas or disciplines, and this can be confusing, particularly for young children. I learned this lesson the first year I taught kindergarten. I was talking to the children about our hundred chart, and I probably said something like, "Which is a *lower* number, 10 (pointing to 10) or 20 (pointing to 20)?" Several children unanimously agreed that 20 was the lower number. Confused, I asked *why* they thought that, and I quickly realized that 20 is physically "lower" down than 10 on the chart.

Hundred Chart

1	2	3	4	5	6	7	8	9	10
11	12	13	14	15	16	17	18	19	20
21	22	23	24	25	26	27	28	29	30
31	32	33	34	35	36	37	38	39	40
41	42	43	44	45	46	47	48	49	50
51	52	53	54	55	56	57	58	59	60
61	62	63	64	65	66	67	68	69	70
71	72	73	74	75	76	77	78	79	80
81	82	83	84	85	86	87	88	89	90
91	92	93	94	95	96	97	98	99	100

When discipline-specific meanings create confusion: 20 is *lower* down on the chart, but 10 is the *lower* number in a math conversation.

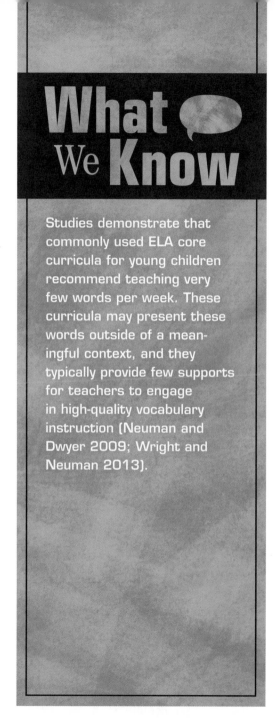

What We Know

Studies demonstrate that commonly used ELA core curricula for young children recommend teaching very few words per week. These curricula may present these words outside of a meaningful context, and they typically provide few supports for teachers to engage in high-quality vocabulary instruction (Neuman and Dwyer 2009; Wright and Neuman 2013).

The children were using a common meaning of the word *lower* that they already knew (put your shoes on the *lower* shelf). However, in mathematical conversations, of course, a *lower* number means a smaller quantity. The everyday meaning of the word led children to a response based on an understanding that was completely different from its mathematical meaning. And, these children would hopefully learn another meaning of *lower* when they went to music class (a *lower* note or *lower* pitch)!

Of course, common words with different, discipline-specific meanings are not just found in math; they pop up in every content area. Consider, for example:

A *legend* on a map is different from a *legend* that is a type of story.

A *front* in weather is different from the *front* of the line.

The *force* in a Star Wars movie has a different meaning from a *force* in physics.

Any time you encounter words like these you will have wonderful opportunities to support children to notice and learn these multiple meanings.

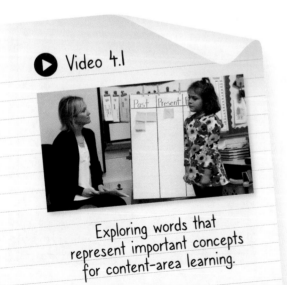

▶ Video 4.1

Exploring words that represent important concepts for content-area learning.

Words Are Tools for Engaging in Learning

As part of a science lesson focused on learning about forces, a group of kindergartners are moving toys and then describing how they made these objects move. Their teacher walks around the classroom and uses questions and prompts to help the children deepen their understanding of new ideas while applying the words *push* and *pull* to their observations.

TEACHER: So how did you make the toys move?

ISAIAH: *Push* them or *pull* them.

TEACHER: What do you mean by that? Tell me more about that.

ISAIAH: Um, people *push* them, then . . .

TEACHER: To make them do what?

ISAIAH: Move.

TEACHER: Move. How do they move when you *push* them?

BRIANNA: It goes over there.

TEACHER: It goes over there. Away from you. And what about *pull*? Would they move the same way if you *pull* them or would they move differently?

BRIANNA: Different.

TEACHER: Different. How would they move differently?

ISAIAH: They would *pull* them backwards [pulls a toy car toward himself].

TEACHER: Backward. So if someone is *pulling* something, can you put your arm out? If someone's *pulling* something [brings hand in toward body] . . . they're moving it closer to themselves. If someone's *pushing* something, try that [pushes hand away from body and students do the same]. They're moving it away.

Before this learning experience, the children could use the words *push* and *pull* (the tip of the iceberg), but now through their exploration and their teacher's prompts and questions, they are deepening their ideas about what these words mean (everything below the surface of the iceberg). The words have become "tools" for learning and communicating in a particular discipline (Nagy and Townsend 2012). When we think of words in this way—as tools for engaging in learning—we realize that vocabulary development for its own sake is not the end goal. Engagement is the goal.

Imagine the conversation above being replaced or preempted by the teacher simply telling children a definition of the words *pull* and *push* and then moving on. Which option seems better aligned with what we know about vocabulary learning? The meaningful context where the words are relevant and useful, of course. Which option seems better aligned with science learning? The one where children manipulate and explore with real objects, of course. Learning new words (and deepening your conceptual knowledge of words) *while* learning new things is better for both language development and science learning. It's a win-win!

Meteorologist

A meteorologist is a scientist who studies the weather and climate.

You May Be Wondering

Q: *Wouldn't it be more efficient to pre-teach all of the vocabulary before starting a unit or topic?*

A: Pre-teaching all of the words for a unit is *not* more efficient because children are unlikely to retain the pre-taught words well enough to use them later in the unit. Remember:

- *We need lots of word meaning information.* When previewing a list of words, it's hard to move beyond a basic definition and maybe an example or a single picture.

- *We learn words that are relevant and useful.* A list of words is just a list of words—neither relevant nor useful.

- *We need exposure in meaningful contexts.* There is no meaningful context because children have not started to engage in the learning of the unit yet.

- *We learn words when we have opportunities for active processing.* Active processing means thinking about the meaning of words or using them to communicate ideas. An out-of-context list doesn't support this.

So, when is the right time to teach discipline-specific vocabulary? It's best to introduce words as children *need* them—as they are thinking, exploring, or engaging with ideas—and the words are relevant and useful.

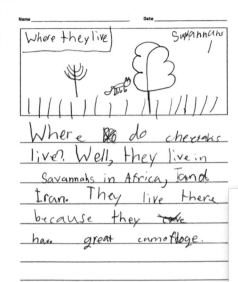

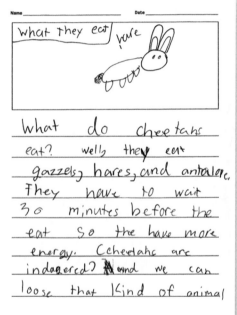

A child has learned a lot about cheetahs from reading books about this fascinating animal. Specialized vocabulary—*savannahs, camouflage, endangered*—helps the child think about the topic in discipline-specific ways.

Plan to Support Vocabulary Development During Content-Area Learning

Now let's think about planning. When you consider the question, "When will it be most relevant and useful for children to learn this word?" you have to think more expansively about your teaching than you would if you planned just to preview words at the beginning of the unit. But if you really want children to learn the words they need to read, write, speak, listen for, and learn during content area learning, the upfront planning is worth the time and effort.

First, Identify the Content You Plan to Teach

Understanding exactly what concepts, knowledge, and practices children need to learn by the end of a unit should always be the first step in planning. To determine this, you might use content-area standards, curriculum materials adopted by your school, or units that teachers have designed. The goal is to understand exactly what you want students to learn—each week and in each lesson—in order to support them to meet content-area learning goals.

Next, Look for Read-Aloud Texts Connected to the Content

Informational books and other texts expand the walls of our classrooms in important ways. They allow children to experience things they cannot discover or manipulate firsthand—things that are too big (a whale), too far away (polar bears), or from different time periods (dinosaurs). They are filled with interesting content and are a great source for new words and vocabulary. While some curricula may recommend or include a few read-aloud texts, when you supplement these materials children have opportunities to learn with informational texts regularly in their classrooms.

Create Informational Text Sets

You have probably had the experience of reading deeply on a topic. Perhaps you wanted to learn something new—say, what's involved in composting, how to tile your shower, or how to help your child sleep through the night—so you read a lot about the topic. Maybe you visited different websites, read a variety of articles and books, or watched videos to learn more. Reading informational texts is a very authentic way to investigate or learn something new.

Or think back to your college courses. Early in the semester, the readings might have felt challenging and confusing, but as you read more, the ideas began to make sense. The concepts that you learned in earlier readings helped you understand later readings. Over time, you became more knowledgeable about the topic and familiar with its associated vocabulary, and it changed the way you read.

Okay, this may be more than a tip. It's *really* important. Remember that reading a book about science is not an acceptable replacement for giving children opportunities to actually *do* science. Why? Well, consider this: Which is more likely to support children's learning—reading a book about the fact that plants need light to grow, or actually growing two plants (one in a dark place and one in light)? The answer seems obvious, but that said, you probably want children to learn more about different types of plants that grow in very different habitats than the plants you are growing in your classroom, and informational texts are your ticket to this learning. The key is, you want children to engage with texts *and* have opportunities to participate in the practices of a discipline. For more, see *No More Science Kits or Texts in Isolation* by Jacqueline Barber and Gina N. Cervetti (2019).

A text set is a set of texts (read-alouds or independent reading texts) that address the same topic and similar concepts. When we read aloud or ask children to read from text sets, they have this same experience. They encounter the same important words that are critical for learning about a concept again and again across the texts, and this natural repetition supports vocabulary development and knowledge building. And when these reading opportunities are integrated with other types of exploration and investigations, children's content-area learning is even more powerful.

This way of thinking about text sets may challenge what you know because often teachers plan for an informational text week or unit where children read informational texts purely to learn *about* informational texts. Here is an example of what the read-alouds might look like for an "informational text" unit (Cervetti, Wright, and Hwang 2016).

Not a Text Set

It's not clear exactly what children are expected to learn over the course of reading these texts. They're not likely to build deep knowledge on any of the books' topics, and they won't gain repeated exposure to the same set of vocabulary.

In contrast, when children are learning about, say, weather forecasting tools (*thermometer, precipitation gauge, wind sock*), the following texts will almost certainly deepen their knowledge and vocabulary about this topic.

Read-Aloud Text Set
for Kindergarten Weather Forecasting Unit

What Is Severe Weather? by Jennifer Boothroyd

What's the Weather? by E.B. Church and D. Ohanesian

I Face the Wind by Vicki Cobb, illustrated by Julia Gorton

Clouds by Erin Edison

The Seasons of Arnold's Apple Tree by Gail Gibbons

What Is Precipitation? by Robin Johnson

Next Time You See a Cloud by Emily Morgan

Is It Hot or Cold? by Carrie Stuart

What We Know

In one study, children were randomly assigned to read either a text set or a set of unrelated informational texts. The children who read the text set built deeper knowledge of the topic, they learned more conceptually-central vocabulary, and they were better at retelling a new text that addressed the same concepts (Cervetti, Wright, and Hwang 2016). These findings suggest that there are benefits to knowledge, vocabulary, and children's comprehension when they read a set of related texts.

Make an Ambitious List of Words to Teach

The next step in planning is to make a list of the words children will need to know as they learn about and discuss the content you plan to teach. Remember that this list is *not* to hand out or preview; it's to help you plan and think about when learning new words will be most helpful to students. And it will be ambitious. This is not a five-new-words-per-week or daily-word approach to teaching vocabulary. It's an all day, all subjects, part-of-every-thing-children-learn approach, so children will be learning a lot of new words.

Here are some questions to ask as you make the list:

Which words will children need to know to meet content-area standards? (E.g., if second-grade science standards focus on how plants move their seeds around, you might want to teach children the term *dispersal*.)

Which words will children need to know to *engage* in a particular unit?

Which words will children need to know to *discuss* new concepts and meet learning goals?

Does my curriculum include a list of words to teach?

Are there important words that are not included in my curriculum?

Are there important words that are used again and again in this content area (e.g., words like *deliberate* or *resource* in social studies or the words *hypothesis* or *observation* in science)?

Are there words that I should review to make sure that all children in the classroom are on the same page? (E.g., if we are discussing the *amount* of cloud cover in the sky, do all children know what the word *amount* means?)

Are there important words that are particular to this topic? (E.g., if children are working on addition, they will need to learn the word *sum*.)

Are there words with specialized meanings in this discipline that could alleviate confusion? (E.g., what does it mean when an equation is *true* in math?)

Are there words in the read-aloud text set that children will need to know?

As an example, here is an ambitious list of over sixty new vocabulary terms for a unit on weather forecasting in kindergarten. When we asked ourselves these questions, we realized children would need to know a lot of words to engage in this unit and to talk about their learning across the lessons that we planned:

Words for a
Weather Forecasting Unit

air	freezing	snowstorm
blow	freezing rain	solid
breezy	hail	spring
balm	hot	stratus
cirrus	hurricane	summer
cloud	ice crystals	sun
cloud cover	liquid	sunny
cloudy	meteorologist	temperature
cold	partly cloudy	thermometer
cool	precipitation	thunderstorm
cumulonimbus	precipitation gauge	tornado
cumulus	rain	warm
fall	season	water droplets
flood	severe	weather conditions
flutter	sleet	wind
forecast	snow	wind speed
		winter

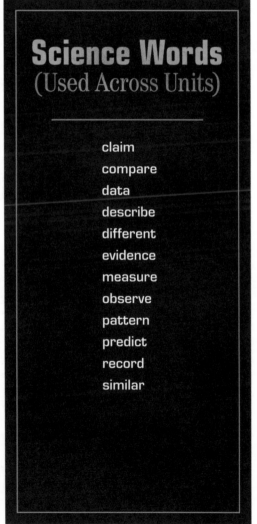

Science Words
(Used Across Units)

- claim
- compare
- data
- describe
- different
- evidence
- measure
- observe
- pattern
- predict
- record
- similar

You May Be Wondering

Q : *Should I have a vocabulary word wall for different content areas?*

A : Good question. It helps to think about the purpose of the word wall and how it will be used. Sometimes words are added to a word wall at the beginning of a unit and then they are just there . . . posted to the wall for the rest of the school year. Children may not use or access the word wall ever again after the word is first added. Sometimes, children can't yet decode the words on the wall, and so they are unable to access these words, even if they wanted to. Overall, if children cannot or are not expected to use the wall as a reference, then it is probably not worth the time and effort to create it.

Word walls *are* a good idea if children are encouraged to refer to the words and can use them to engage in reading, writing, and speaking. However, this doesn't always require a physical wall. Words to reference can live in a binder, on chart paper, or any sort of shared document. You might put an image or photograph next to a word to help children recognize it if they can't decode it.

Consider When and How You Will Teach the Words

You will need to consider which words you will teach during which lessons, of course, but also *when* during the lessons you will teach them. To decide this, I always ask myself, "When will children need this language in order to think and talk about the ideas that they are learning? When will it be most relevant and useful?"

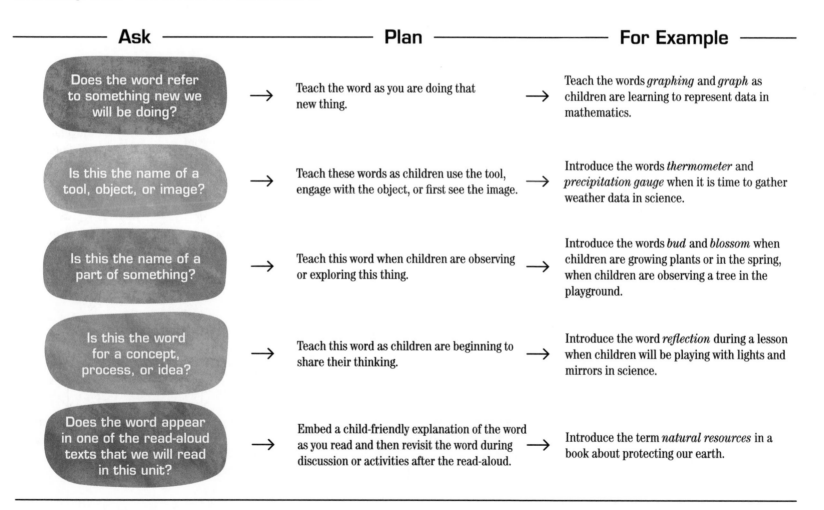

Ask	Plan	For Example
Does the word refer to something new we will be doing? →	Teach the word as you are doing that new thing. →	Teach the words *graphing* and *graph* as children are learning to represent data in mathematics.
Is this the name of a tool, object, or image? →	Teach these words as children use the tool, engage with the object, or first see the image. →	Introduce the words *thermometer* and *precipitation gauge* when it is time to gather weather data in science.
Is this the name of a part of something? →	Teach this word when children are observing or exploring this thing. →	Introduce the words *bud* and *blossom* when children are growing plants or in the spring, when children are observing a tree in the playground.
Is this the word for a concept, process, or idea? →	Teach this word as children are beginning to share their thinking. →	Introduce the word *reflection* during a lesson when children will be playing with lights and mirrors in science.
Does the word appear in one of the read-aloud texts that we will read in this unit? →	Embed a child-friendly explanation of the word as you read and then revisit the word during discussion or activities after the read-aloud. →	Introduce the term *natural resources* in a book about protecting our earth.

Vocabulary Planning Chart for a Unit Lesson

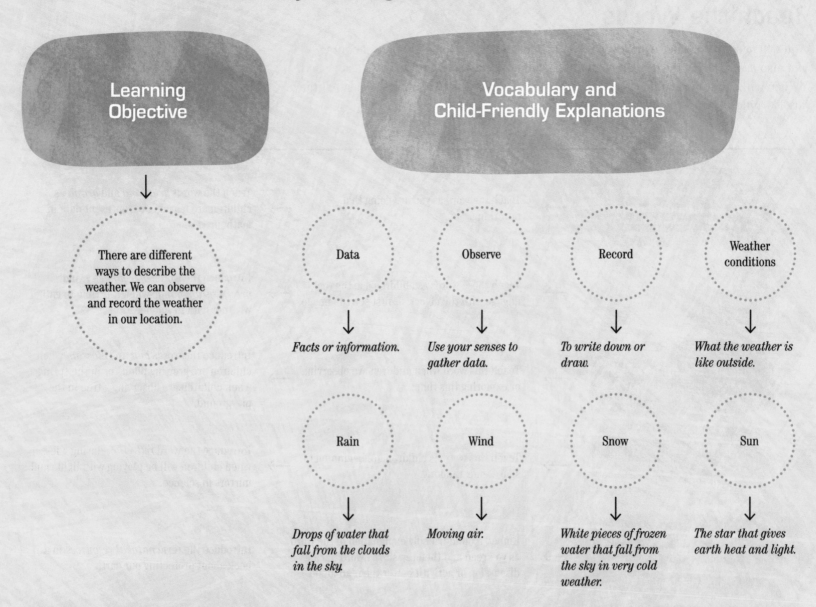

Learning Objective

There are different ways to describe the weather. We can observe and record the weather in our location.

Vocabulary and Child-Friendly Explanations

Data

Facts or information.

Observe

Use your senses to gather data.

Record

To write down or draw.

Weather conditions

What the weather is like outside.

Rain

Drops of water that fall from the clouds in the sky.

Wind

Moving air.

Snow

White pieces of frozen water that fall from the sky in very cold weather.

Sun

The star that gives earth heat and light.

When will I introduce new vocabulary?

↓

During read-aloud,
What's the Weather?
weather conditions,
rain, wind, snow, sun.

↓

While showing
materials right before
outdoor observation of
weather conditions:
observe, data, record.

When will children have opportunities to use these words in a meaningful context?

↓

Children
will go outside
to observe weather
conditions on a recording
sheet with space to
draw and write or
label.

↓

Questions
to ask while
children observe:
*What do you observe about
the weather conditions?*
How did you observe this?
*What data are you recording
about the weather
conditions?*

Encourage Children to Use New Words . . .

When They Discuss Books, Ideas, and Content

Talking about new content we are learning, especially after engaging with it, is one of the most powerful ways to actively process new words. Here are a few simple facilitation moves you can use again and again to support children to use the new words you are teaching them as they talk.

──── **Facilitation Moves** ──────── **For Example** ────────

Respond to what children say using new vocabulary.

> **CHILD:** It's cold.

> **TEACHER:** You *observed* that your body feels cold outside today.

Invite children to add to what they say.

> **CHILD:** It's cold.

> **TEACHER:** You *observed* that your body feels cold outside today. What else did you *observe*?

Encourage children to be more precise.

> **CHILD:** There are *some clouds* in the sky today.

> **TEACHER:** How would a meteorologist say *some clouds*?

Use sentence stems.

> **TEACHER:** Can we each start by saying, "Today, I *observed* . . . " and then share what you *recorded*?

Sentence stems help children use new vocabulary in authentic ways.

What I still wonder about Matter

Do gases evaporate?

Why do solids break?

Is light matter?

How does heat evaporate water?

Students' questions show they are deepening their conceptual knowledge about matter.

After writing about their past, present, and future lives, children use sentence stems to talk to each other about their ideas.

 Speaker

· In the past I...

· In the present I...

· In the future I hope to...

· Some things that have changed are...

☺ Listener 👂

One thing I'm wondering about your _____ is...

· past
· present
· future

Talking about new content we are learning, especially after engaging with it, is one of the most powerful ways to actively process new words.

When They Write

When children write, they have a fantastic opportunity to use new words and actively process their meanings. Once children have learned new vocabulary associated with content they are learning, encourage them to include these words in their writing.

Jonathan uses lots of specific vocabulary, such as *predict*, *minerals*, *soot*, and *toxic*, to describe volcanoes when his class learns about processes that shape the earth.

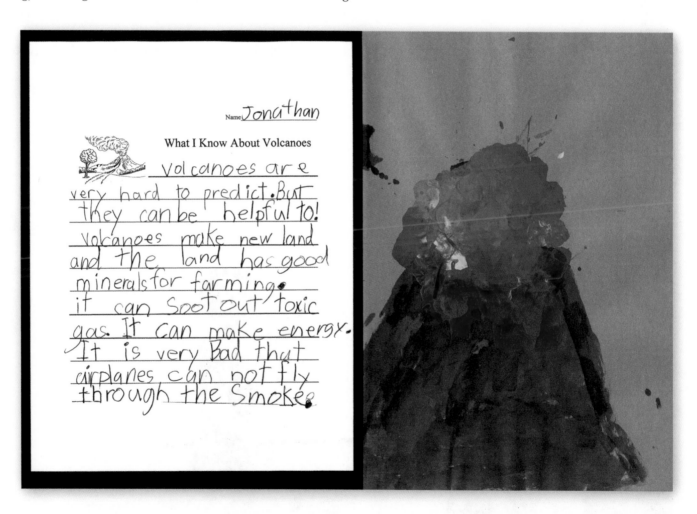

Name: Jonathan

What I Know About Volcanoes

volcanoes are very hard to predict. But they can be helpful to! volcanoes make new land and the land has good minerals for farming. it can soot out toxic gas. It can make energy. It is very Bad that airplanes can not fly through the Smoke.

In Word and Concept Sorts

Sorting, organizing, or categorizing pictures, items, or words is a great way for kids to process the words and organize the ideas that they are learning. Imagine, for example, a stack of laminated photos showing different modes of transportation. One child might sort the images by those that move on land, in water, or through the air. Another child might just as reasonably sort the same images by the number of wheels. Ask children to figure out how they will categorize, and then have them explain their thinking using the new words they have learned.

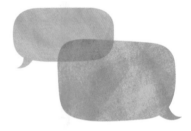

Children sort pictures as they explore the concept of *harvest*.

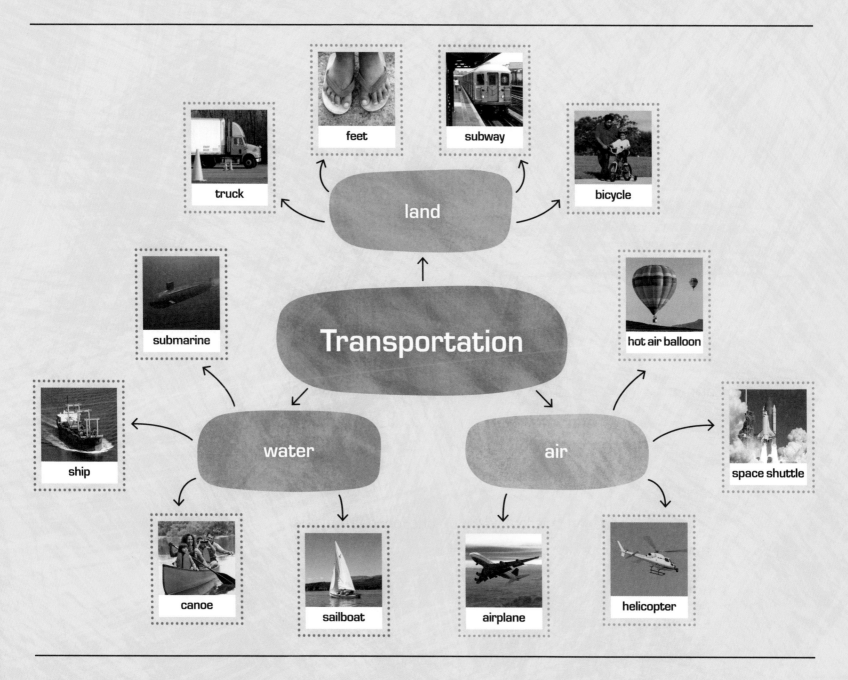

Assess Children's Vocabulary Learning

The best way to know if children are learning new vocabulary is to look and listen for evidence as they talk or write about their learning. To collect these data, consider creating a checklist with the words you've taught across the top and children's names down the side.

Observation Form

	Observe	Data	Weather Conditions
Carmen C.	9/15 sharing with class	9/22 second journal observation	
Rachid A.	9/15 one-on-one outside	9/15 one-on-one outside	
Emma Z.			

Keep the form with you, and when you hear or see children use a new word, record the date and the context where they used it. This creates a helpful "snapshot" of vocabulary learning. You can easily see if there are important words children are *not* using and then offer more support to develop their knowledge of these word meanings. In this class, for example, children were not using the term *weather conditions*. The concept may not have been meaningful or relevant yet to their learning, so it would make sense to talk about why they might be interested in the *weather conditions* on a particular day (because it helps them plan which clothes to wear).

Also, if there are particular students like Emma with dates listed for very few of the words, you will know that these children may need more support or that you may need to check in with them to make sure they understand the new words and concepts you are teaching.

Transportation

Ways of moving from one place to another. Driving a car, going on a bus, or walking can all be types of transportation.

Tip!

Here are some ideas to get you started.

- **Start by planning just one unit.** It can be overwhelming to think about adding vocabulary into everything you teach, but it is okay to start small so you don't feel overwhelmed by the task.

- **Team up.** Consider working with colleagues at the same grade level to create your content-area vocabulary lists together. That way, children across all classrooms at a grade level will have the opportunity to learn lots of relevant new vocabulary as they learn new content.

- **Save your work!** You can use your plans to support children's vocabulary development again next year—a one-time effort with long-term benefits.

You May Be Wondering

Q: *I'm concerned that my students just aren't developmentally ready to learn all of these big fancy words. Some of them barely know basic words like* sofa.

A: First, if you have determined that your students don't know the meaning of the word *sofa* or any other words that seem important to daily life in your classroom, by all means, help them to learn these words. Just remember that some children may not have been exposed to that particular word if their family calls it a *couch* or if they don't happen to own a sofa.

That said, there is no "correct" developmental order for learning words. Some types of learning build upon one another, but this is not the case for vocabulary learning. Remember that we learn words that are relevant and useful when we are exposed to those words in meaningful contexts. So, if we use big words with children in meaningful ways across the school day, those are the words that children will learn. Put simply, it is fine to learn both the word *sofa* and the word *evidence* on the same day if these are both useful for children's learning!

Finally, don't shy away from high expectations. Children love to learn big fancy words and to use these words to discuss and describe their ideas, their feelings, and their world. Words are powerful tools, and we can offer these powerful tools to children, no matter which words they currently know or do not yet know.

Learn More

Baker, S. et al. 2014. *Teaching Academic Content and Literacy to English Learners in Elementary and Middle School.* NCEE 2014-4012. Washington, DC: U.S. Department of Education, National Center for Education Evaluation and Regional Assistance (NCEE), Institute of Education Sciences. https://ies.ed.gov/ncee/wwc/PracticeGuide/19.

Gotwals, A. W., and T. Wright. 2017. "From 'Plants Don't Eat' to 'Plants Are Producers': The Role of Vocabulary in Scientific Sense-Making." *Science and Children* 55(3): 44–50.

SOLID Start. 2020. *SOLID Start Curriculum: Weather Forecasting Unit.* Michigan State University College of Education. http://solidstart.msu.edu.

Wright, T. S., and A. W. Gotwals. 2017a. "Supporting Disciplinary Talk from the Start of School: Teaching Students to Think and Talk Like Scientists." *The Reading Teacher* 71(2): 189–97.

Wright, et al. 2019. "Discussion Supports Sense-Making Within and Across Lessons." *Science and Children* 57(4): 50–56.

5

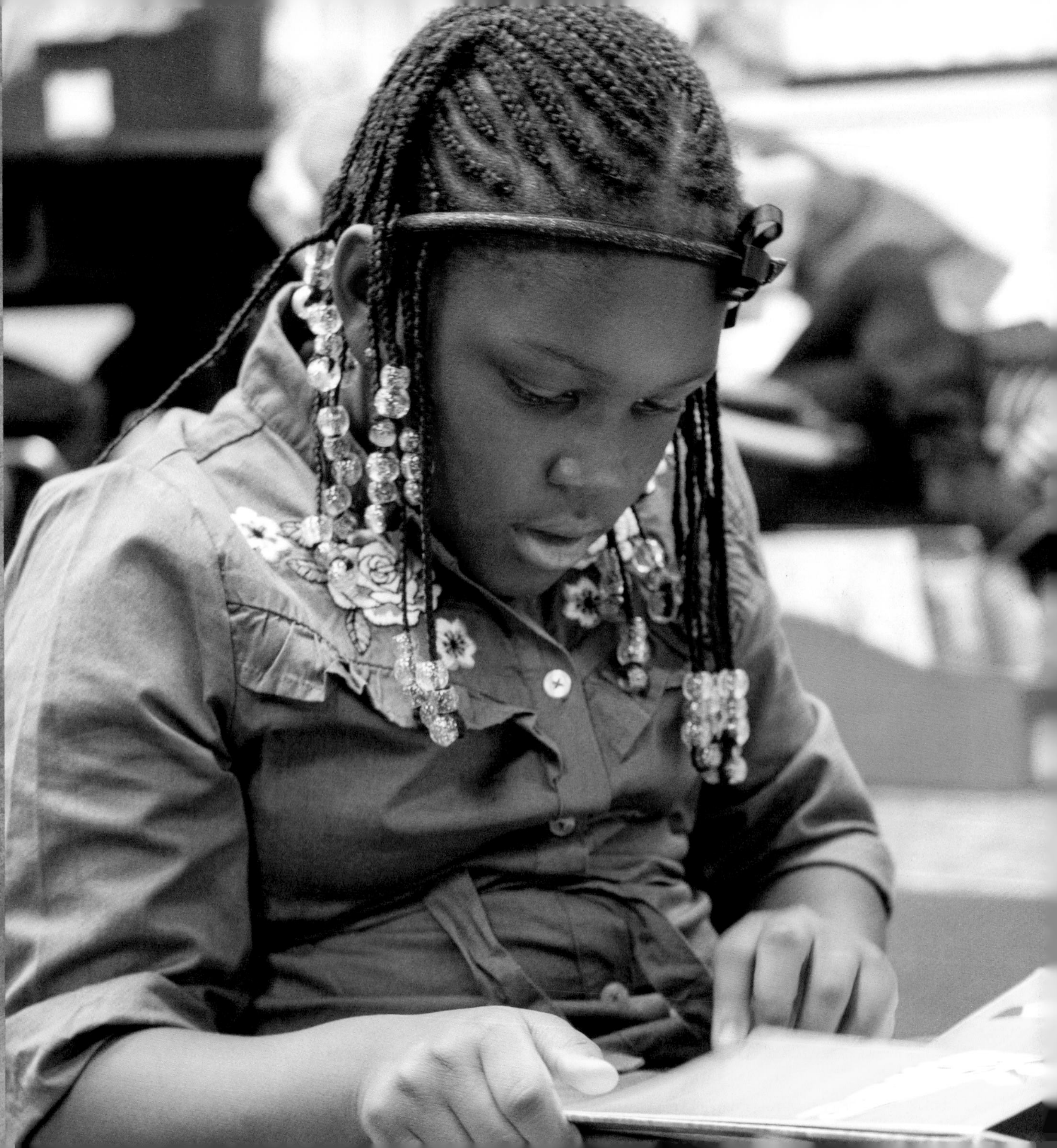

Vocabulary Development During Reading Instruction

When my daughter was in third grade, she told me about a text that she felt she had not understood well on a standardized reading assessment. When I asked if she remembered what it was about, she responded that it was about knights and squires, but she pronounced the word *squire* with a schwa rather than the long /I/ sound. So, the word sounded like *squir* at the beginning of *squirrel*. Clearly, she hadn't heard the word *squire* before and she didn't know its meaning, so she couldn't map the letters and sounds she saw on the page onto a word that was already in her oral vocabulary.

After sharing the correct pronunciation, I asked her if she had learned what a *squire* was from her reading, and she was able to tell me that she had figured out that "a squire is a helper to a knight." Even though she had not decoded the word correctly, she had been able to understand enough of the other words in the text to figure out some meaning for this unknown word.

If a reader understands most of the words in a text, the text itself may provide a meaningful context that gives information about a new word. Reading *a lot*, over time, provides many opportunities for incidental vocabulary learning, particularly if the same word is encountered repeatedly across texts and over time. If we are truly committed to supporting vocabulary development across the day, then, it's critical that we support children as they engage in lots of independent reading.

Supported Independent Reading

As teachers, we want children to read a lot. We want them to read challenging texts, and we don't want them to quit because the vocabulary gate is closed. Have you ever seen a child pick up an exciting new book that they really want to read, but they encounter several words with meanings they don't know on the first few pages? On top of doing the very hard work of learning to decode text, that child feels a lot like you did when you read the bosonic theory paragraph earlier in the book—confused and not very motivated to keep reading. Who wants to look at the lines and squiggles on a page and say words that do not make sense?

Since we know that reading is an important context for vocabulary learning, and we know that children need to read to become better readers, we need to make time for our students to read every day and also think very intentionally about how to keep the vocabulary gate open as they do. Let's explore some ideas for how to make that happen.

You May Be Wondering

Q: *What is the relationship between text level and vocabulary?*

A: Typically, calculations of text level are based on word difficulty and syntactic complexity. Word difficulty is typically calculated by word frequency (i.e., words that occur less frequently in written text increase the text level) or word length (i.e., longer words increase the text level).

If you take a text and paste it into an online readability calculator, and then you take all of the common words and trade them out for more challenging vocabulary, the text level will go up. If you take all of the challenging words and replace them with more common or shorter synonyms, the text level will go down. Like this:

> One night, I took my dog for a walk. We walked to the store. I was thirsty so I got a drink. Then we walked home. I had a very good night with my dog. (Flesch-Kincaid Grade Level: Below first grade)

> At twilight, I took my Weimaraner for a stroll. We sauntered to the supermarket. I was parched so I purchased a beverage. I had an absolutely delightful evening with my pooch. (Flesch-Kincaid Grade Level: Sixth grade)

So, as children read more challenging texts, they will encounter more difficult vocabulary.

Include a Variety of Texts in the Classroom

It's hard to know what will hook a child on reading, particularly because it can be really slow going and "not that fun" when children are first slugging through decoding text. The more options we have available in our classrooms, the more likely we are to find that magical text that makes reading feel wonderful and possible for a particular child. I still remember the moment when one of my daughters, who loves art, discovered graphic novels, beginning with the Elephant and Piggie series by Mo Willems. She worked her way through every book in that series and then moved on to read every graphic novel we could find for young children.

Finding those magical texts is so important for young readers. And each child is different, so it is important to provide lots of options.

Get to know children and their interests to help match them with texts they might enjoy. Consider using a reading interest inventory at the beginning of the year so that children can quickly let you know what they might want to read.

Include a range of genres, authors, and topics, and both fiction and informational texts.

If you cannot purchase a range of texts, bring in books from the library.

Include texts that represent children's cultural backgrounds, experiences, and interests. Remember that readers comprehend more (and can read more challenging text) when they have background knowledge that is aligned with the text.

Build Enthusiasm for Reading

If we want children to read a lot, then our classrooms should feel like places where reading is something we choose to do because it's just so satisfying and fun. To help build that feeling:

- Highlight texts with brief text introductions. "I want to tell you about this wonderful book in our library," or "Guess what? We just received the new edition of *Ranger Rick*!" or "I found the most interesting website you might want to read."

- Create a "Favorite Texts" space where children can share recommendations. Sometimes knowing a friend loves reading a particular book or series can be motivating for children.

- Do not limit children to reading texts only at a particular level. If children are interested in a book or a topic, they may be willing to work through a more challenging text than you would expect. Recent studies demonstrate that children grow as readers when they read challenging texts with scaffolding and support (O'Connor, Swanson, and Geraghty 2010).

Encourage Children to Read Text Sets on Topics of Interest

Remember that challenging words and concepts become easier the more we learn about them, so reading five or six informational books on the same topic helps with incidental word learning as children encounter the same words repeatedly across the texts.

When you support a child by offering a text set, consider the order. For example, if a child wants to read a challenging text about outer space but doesn't yet know a lot of concepts and vocabulary related to this topic, you might suggest they first listen to an audio book about space and then start with a few less challenging texts on the topic before moving to the more complex texts that they are excited to read. The idea is to ramp up the difficulty of texts, allowing the child to learn key vocabulary and concepts over time and build toward reading the more challenging text.

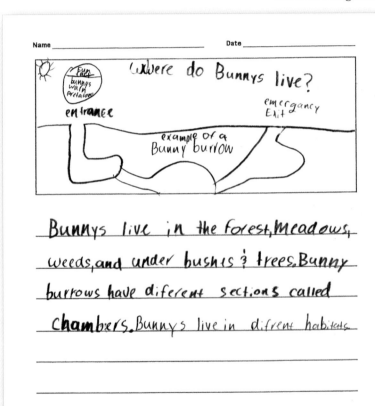

Children in this class have each chosen an animal to study to learn more about the concept of habitats. This child encountered words such as *burrows*, *chambers*, and *habitats* multiple times in a text set of books about rabbits.

A Teacher's Guide to Vocabulary Development Across the Day

Have Children Read to Gather Information

Just as we can read aloud across all content areas during the day, children can also read independently to support their learning in all content areas—not just during "reading time." Maybe children are learning about how animals survive in different habitats in science or learning about geographic regions in their state during social studies. Let them read to gather information and learn more about these important topics.

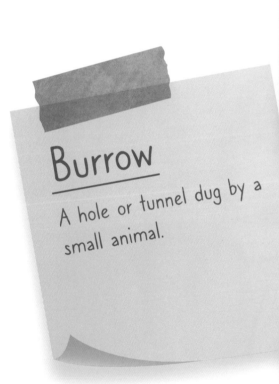

Burrow

A hole or tunnel dug by a small animal.

As they are reading independently, invite children to use sticky notes to mark words they don't understand and can't really figure out from context. You can refer to these notes when you meet with them one-on-one, or you might ask children to share interesting words they've encountered in their reading and talk about them with other children.

Coach Children as They Read

When children are reading independently, teachers are not off duty. This is an important time to discuss texts with children in one-on-one settings (sometimes called coaching or conferring) or to provide instruction to a small group.

To check in with children about vocabulary, ask them if there are words or ideas they don't understand. If the vocabulary is causing challenges for comprehension, discussing these words or concepts can open the vocabulary gate for children. After discussing a word, always go back to where it appears in the text to make sure the overall meaning is now clear.

Extend Reading Beyond the School Day

Do whatever you can to make sure that children have texts they *want to read* after school, at home, and during school breaks. You might:

★ Take your class to the school library.

★ Help children get library cards so they can borrow books from the public library.

★ Loan children books from your classroom library.

★ Organize book swaps where families send in used books they no longer want and each child "shops" for books to take home.

★ Recommend websites that are appropriate for children to read online at home.

Whole Class Minilessons

Most teachers who set aside time each day for children to read independently support that reading with short, focused minilessons. In minilessons, we cover a range of strategies and skills that readers need to grow—including learning about vocabulary. So, in addition to building children's curiosity and interest in language during read-alouds, minilessons reinforce these ideas when children are doing the reading.

Because children are reading different books in independent reading, you won't be focusing on specific words in your minilessons. Instead, you'll offer children information about how words work and strategies to deal with the unknown words they will encounter as they read. Let's consider both now.

Teach Children *About* Words

The more children understand about how our language works, the better equipped they will be to figure out word meanings on their own. But what do they need to know? Well, just a few important ideas go a long way, and it's a good idea to revisit them across the year in your minilessons:

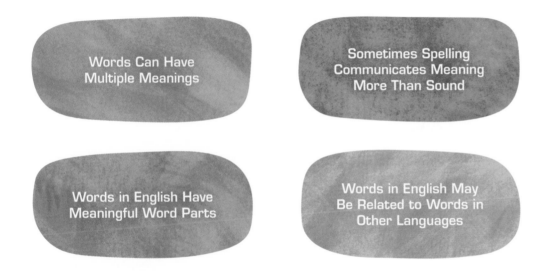

Words Can Have Multiple Meanings

Sometimes Spelling Communicates Meaning More Than Sound

Words in English Have Meaningful Word Parts

Words in English May Be Related to Words in Other Languages

When you come across examples of words that illustrate these understandings, simply add them to running lists and talk about how they deepen everyone's understanding of each important idea. Here's a little explanation of each one.

Words Can Have Multiple Meanings

Take the word *shower*, for instance. In its noun form, it could be a passing rain shower, the shower in your bathroom, or a baby shower for your friend who's expecting a baby. But *shower* can also be a verb—you can shower someone with kindness, or shower yourself after a long, sweaty run. Help children understand that if a word doesn't make sense when they are reading, maybe it's because the author is using a different meaning of that word. To explore this idea further, you might read and laugh at examples from Amelia Bedelia books. In *Play Ball*, for example, Amelia fills home "plate" with cookies and when the kids yell for her to run "home," she runs all the way back to her house!

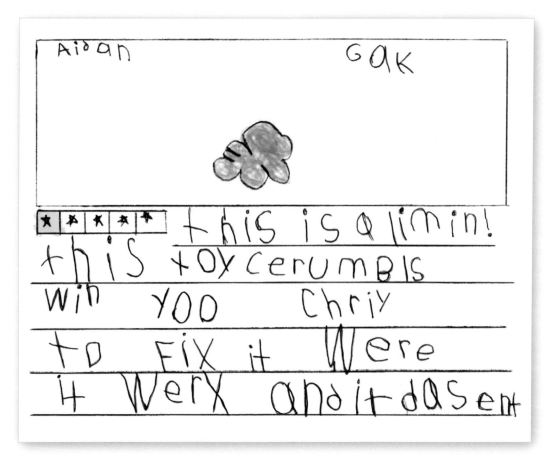

In this toy review, a child shows he knows that a *lemon* can be something other than just a sour fruit—it also means something that doesn't work well! *This is a lemon! This toy crumbles when you try to fix it. . . .*

A Teacher's Guide to Vocabulary Development Across the Day

Sometimes Spelling Communicates Meaning More Than Sound

When you decode a word, sometimes it sounds like another word you know, but if the spelling is different, the meaning is different. Take the words *bear* and *bare*, for instance. A child might read, "The tree was *bare*" and map that word onto an image of a big, hairy animal, a *bear*. Examples of this abound—inn/in, boar/bore, currant/current, morning/mourning, scents/sense, cheep/cheap, ware/where, to/too/two, etc. You can also get inspired by sharing puns (which are funny because they exploit the different possible meanings of words that sound alike) you find on the internet or in books.

Where do polar bears vote?
The North Poll.

Insect puns bug me.

What makes music on your hair?
A head band.

What do you call a dinosaur with a big vocabulary?
A thesaurus.

Name _____ Date _____

how they hunt

70mph   zoomin

Next, I'm going to teach you about how they hunt. Cheetahs uasully stalk their prey. If they get away, no problem. Chetahs use their claws and tails to catch up. They can go about 70mph. Then they jump on their prey, and kill their prey using their sharp claws again.

Prey **sounds just like** *pray,* **of course, but they mean something very different.**

Tip!

Word meanings *always* matter. Sometimes, when we are teaching letter-sound relationships, we forget that children may not know the meanings of the words we use as examples. Whenever I see children who are learning the short /o/ sound, for instance, I always ask if they know what *bog* and *hog* actually mean. Often, they do not.

The focus of all reading and writing instruction should always be on making meaning, even when we are teaching skills. We do not decode just for the sake of decoding. Whether children are building words, sorting spelling patterns or pictures, or learning particular letter-sound combinations, remember to make time to discuss word meanings as part of this instruction.

Words in English Have Meaningful Word Parts

Prefixes, suffixes, and roots have meanings. If you see the prefix *un-* in a word, for example, you know that whatever the rest of the word means, it's *not*, in this case—*unclean, undo, unfair*. And if you can figure out the meaning of parts of a word, you might be able to figure out something about what the whole word means. This doesn't always work perfectly, of course. In a discussion about the word *extinct*, for example, I once heard a child surmise that it's "like when a skunk is out of its spray. It is out of stink." This student knew that one meaning of the prefix *ex-* is "out of" or "without" and he applied this to a new word. It didn't quite work, but it is the type of smart thinking about how words work that we want to encourage!

Words in English May Be Related to Words in Other Languages

The word *celebration* in English is *celebración* in Spanish, and the word *curious* is *curioso*. Understanding these connections can be very helpful, especially for multilingual students. But just like word parts, cognates sometimes can be misleading. A word might sound similar to a word in a different language, but because it does not have the same root or origin, it can have a very different meaning. For example, *blanco* in Spanish means *white*, not *blank*, and *carta* means a *letter*, not a *card*. Multilingual children may be able to use what they know in one language to figure out the meanings of new words in another language.

Explain and Model Vocabulary Strategies

In your reading minilessons, you probably already teach children decoding strategies (ways to help themselves when they get to a word they don't recognize automatically) and comprehension strategies (ways to help themselves when they don't understand the meaning of a text). But one reason children may not understand the meaning of a text is that there are word meanings they do not know. Vocabulary strategies can help them when they get to an unknown word, but first you have to teach children to notice when they are not understanding *because* of an unknown word. Teach children to look out for this possibility by modeling this thinking during read-alouds:

Is there a word in this text that I do not understand?

Is this making the text confusing for me?

Am I not understanding because I need to figure out a word meaning?

As children get better at knowing when an unknown word is getting in the way of comprehension, you can explain and model vocabulary strategies like these for figuring those words out, and then support children to use them in their independent reading.

▶ Video 5.1

Using context clues to figure out an unknown word.

Look for Context Clues

Show children how sometimes they can use the words they do know in a text to figure out a word they don't know. For example, in *Chrysanthemum*, by Kevin Henkes, the text says, "She did not think her name was absolutely perfect. She thought it was absolutely dreadful." If you do not know what the word *dreadful* means, at least you can figure out that it is the opposite of *absolutely perfect*. Of course, this only works if the text provides this type of information for a challenging word. Invite children to be "detectives" and see if they can find clues in the text to figure out word meanings.

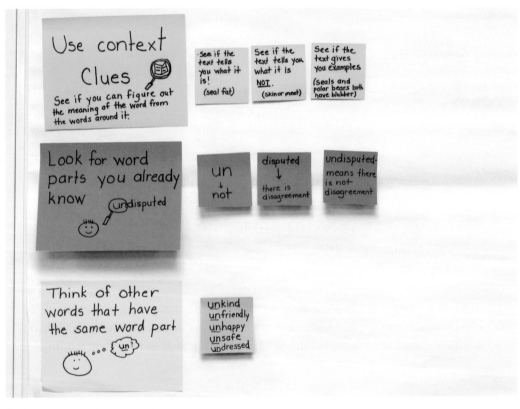

A class chart shows students are learning word-solving strategies.

Remember That Words Have Multiple Meanings

Sometimes children are confused by words they think they know, so it's important to remind them that words have different meanings. A child who only knows *horse* as an animal may be confused by a text that says, "Mom told us not to horse around or we'd get hurt." Teach children to ask, "Could this word have a different meaning that I don't know?" Also, remember that a different spelling for a word that sounds familiar is a signal for a different meaning—you don't want to eat a carat, but you might want to wear one!

Use Known Word Parts to Figure Out Unknown Meanings

Encourage children to use word parts as clues to figure out at least some of the meaning of the word—after all, some meaning is better than no meaning when a tricky word is making it hard to comprehend a text. For example, knowing that a character experiencing *claustrophobia* is afraid of something (*phobia*), even if you're not sure what they are afraid of, is better than not knowing anything at all about the word. Remind children that they can combine word-part knowledge with other context clues to help figure out as much as they can about a word's meaning.

Try a Children's Dictionary or Click on the Definition

"Look it up in the dictionary" is never a good method of vocabulary *instruction*, and a dictionary definition usually doesn't offer enough information to really know a word meaning in-depth. However, dictionaries might provide just enough information to figure out the broader meaning of the text. Wordsmyth.net is a free online dictionary that includes beginner and intermediate definitions that can be useful for children, and some eReaders include features that allow children to click on a word in the text to see a brief definition or synonym. Show children how to use these resources when the meaning of a word makes it hard to understand a text.

Tip!

Be sure to teach children to be *strategic* as they read. Individual vocabulary strategies may not always work for a particular word in a particular text, so it's okay to try several different strategies. Teach children to say, "That's one thing I could try," and then if it doesn't work, "What else can I try?"

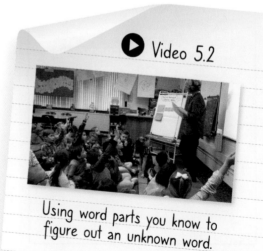

▶ Video 5.2

Using word parts you know to figure out an unknown word.

Ask a Friend or Grown-Up for Help

We all need help sometimes. If children have tried some independent strategies and an unknown word is still preventing them from understanding the text, they can ask someone for help. Remember, the ultimate goal is to comprehend the text, not to be a really great word-solver. If the most efficient way to move forward is simply to ask someone what a word means, then sometimes it's best to just go ahead and ask!

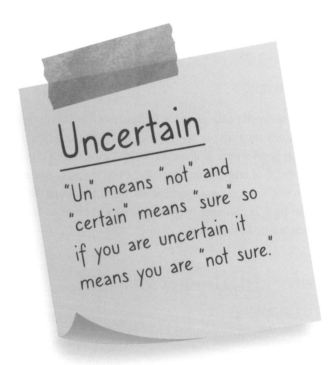

Uncertain

"Un" means "not" and "certain" means "sure" so if you are uncertain it means you are "not sure."

Small-Group Reading Instruction

We know that explaining the meanings of words can open the vocabulary gate for children, but when children are reading independently, it is impossible to preview all the challenging words in every text children select to read. However, teachers often work with small groups in book clubs, inquiry circles, or groups formed to support particular instructional needs. Typically, for small-group instruction, we choose a text to read and discuss that is more challenging than the children in the group can read independently. In these cases, it's important to plan ahead to explain and discuss words that may cause challenges for comprehension.

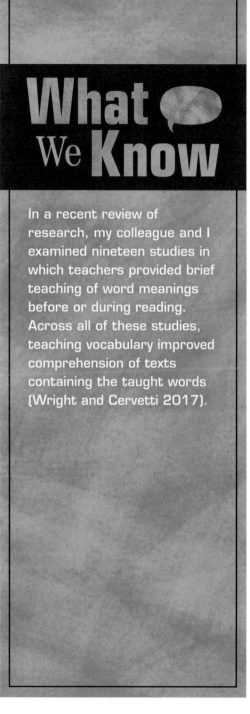

What We Know

In a recent review of research, my colleague and I examined nineteen studies in which teachers provided brief teaching of word meanings before or during reading. Across all of these studies, teaching vocabulary improved comprehension of texts containing the taught words (Wright and Cervetti 2017).

Previewing words is a great way to give young children access to texts that are exciting and interesting to them but may be just a little out of reach (from a meaning-making perspective). Watch the video of Holly Bella previewing words with a small group, then consider the process she uses, which is a lot like the one for supporting vocabulary development during read-aloud.

1

Select words that children may not know *and* that are important for comprehension of the text. This is particularly important if the text does not provide an explanation, example, or adequate context to clarify the meaning of the word.

2

Because children will be reading on their own at different paces within the group, discuss the words you've selected *before* children read the text: "Let's discuss some interesting words that you are going to see when you read today."

3

Show children each word so they can see how they are spelled and practice pronouncing them. This helps them both decode new words and know their meanings.

▶ Video 5.3

A teacher previews words before children read a selection from *Mercy Watson.*

A Teacher's Guide to Vocabulary Development Across the Day

Invite children to share what they know about the words. For example, the small group in the video is discussing the phrase "crisis of an uncertain nature," and Holly invites children to share their understanding of the word *nature*: "Has anyone ever heard the word *nature*? What do you think it means?"

Plan child-friendly explanations for how the words will be used in the text, then guide children toward the explanations (if they don't already know the meaning). Holly's students know that *nature* means relating to the outdoors or things that are not made by people, but Holly explains that in this case, the word *nature* has a different meaning: "It means a kind or type of thing. So, if I said, 'I like candy and cakes and other sweets of that nature.' It means that type or that kind of thing."

Before children start to read, remind them to notice how these words are used in the text as they read. Ask children to think about how understanding the meanings of these words helps them to understand the text.

Remind children to use their vocabulary strategies if they get to an unfamiliar word that you haven't discussed. If they can't figure it out, ask them to mark it to discuss when the group gets back together to talk more about that part of the text.

Tip!

Here are two things you can do right away to get started supporting children's vocabulary development during reading instruction:

- Invite children to look for words they don't understand as they read next week. A first step for word solving is to know that you don't know what a word means and that this might be causing difficulties in comprehending a text.

- Start to teach children about how words work. The more information children have about how words and language work, the more powerful they will feel as strategic word-solvers.

You May Be Wondering

Q: *Wait a moment, didn't you say earlier that teachers should not preview word lists?*

A: Great question and good catch! When we are reading aloud with children, it doesn't make sense to preview many words because we can stop and help children with a word right in the meaningful context where it appears. We can follow up by returning to the page and discussing the word meaning in more depth. When reading aloud, the only words that make sense to preview are those that are not easily explained using a brief child-friendly explanation in context. Similarly, in content-area learning, we can provide or deepen word meaning information as children engage in learning.

But reading groups are a bit different. There are typically four to six children in a group and they are each reading the challenging text at their own pace, so there's no way to open the vocabulary gate for each of them at just the right moment. In this particular case, the best way to support children's vocabulary development is to preview important words in the text they are about to read.

For a longer chapter book, be sure to preview important words as close to the meaningful context as possible by discussing them right before children read the chapter where they will appear.

The more information
children have about how
words and language work,
the more powerful they
will feel as strategic
word-solvers.

Vocabulary Development During Writing Instruction

Word choice is critical for writing. Depending on the genre, we may want children to use words to convince, to describe, to explain, or to convey emotion. We want children to feel like writers, using precise words to share ideas. When children write, they have the opportunity to use and practice all the fantastic words that they know.

Yet, writing poses a different type of vocabulary challenge: Children cannot write using words that they do not know well enough to use in their expressive language. They may know some information about words—just enough to comprehend what is meant when they listen or read. But to use a word in speech or in writing, children need enough information to understand that it is the appropriate word to use.

In this short section, let's consider just a few ways you can support children to use the words they are learning as they write.

PeGoWS WODL.

Think about how precise the very descriptive verb _waddle_ is and how much it shows this beginning writer knows about penguins.

Create Opportunities for Writing Across the Day

If you are supporting children's vocabulary development across the day, then children should have opportunities to use new words to write all day long and not just when it's "time for writing."

Children can use writing to . . .

Plan their work

★ Plan an experiment during science, plan contributions for a text-based discussion

Make predictions

★ Predict what will happen in a story or what will happen in an engineering project

Gather information

★ Write observations or notes on what they are learning

Record an interview

★ Interview a friend or family member to learn about life when they were young, about a job or hobby, about an experience, etc.

Share their thinking

★ Explain how you figured out this math problem or made sense of this science phenomenon

Convince someone to make a change

★ Write to improve something in your school or community

Explain how to do something

★ Record the steps for making something or doing something as a resource for classmates

Say thank you

★ Write notes to helpers in your home, school, or community

As children write across the day in all these ways, make sure to teach the vocabulary they will need to engage in these writing experiences. Also, encourage children to use words you have taught during read-alouds and content-area learning as they write.

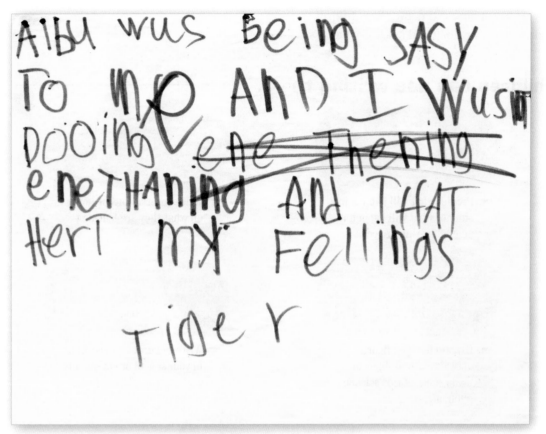

In her kindergarten classroom, Tiger's teacher asks children to write out a grievance, if they have one, rather than tattling. She encourages them to be specific with their words: "Alba was being *sassy*."

A Teacher's Guide to Vocabulary Development Across the Day

Teach Genre-Specific Words

As you read mentor texts to consider text structures for particular genres, look for key
words and phrases that are associated with the genre.

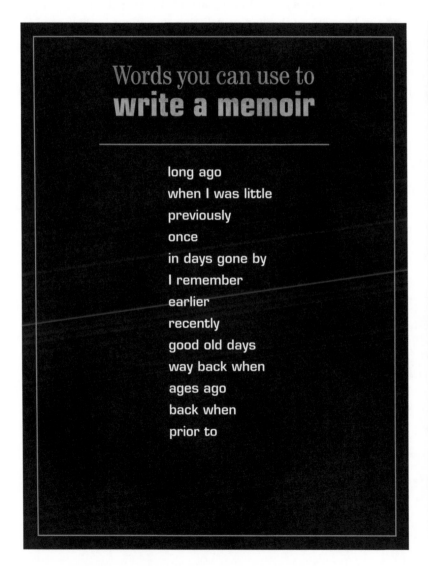

Words you can use to
write a memoir

long ago

when I was little

previously

once

in days gone by

I remember

earlier

recently

good old days

way back when

ages ago

back when

prior to

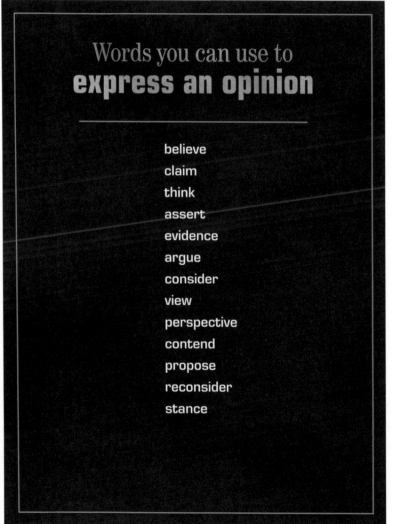

Words you can use to
express an opinion

believe

claim

think

assert

evidence

argue

consider

view

perspective

contend

propose

reconsider

stance

Encourage Spelling Approximations

If you focus on "correct" spelling, children will only write words they can spell correctly. And let's face it, young children will not know the correct spelling for most of the vocabulary we have been discussing in this book. But if you encourage spelling approximations, children can write and use any of the "big" words that they know in their expressive oral language. Encourage children to spell the word the way it sounds so they can express their ideas—and then celebrate when they do (not all children will be comfortable with this at first and will need encouragement). After all, kindergartners who write "excudi" for *excited* or "movftr" for *movie theater* are courageously sharing ideas, using the spelling information they have at their disposal.

Wolves mate to reproduce. This child uses spelling approximations for new vocabulary including *mate* and *reproduce.*

Encourage Meaning Approximations Too!

When children first use a new word in writing or in speech, they may not use it accurately. For example, a third-grade teacher was reading aloud the chapter "Perfidy Unlimited" in Kate DiCamillo's *The Tale of Despereaux*, and her class discussed the meaning of the word *perfidy* (an act of purposeful disloyalty or treachery). The next day, as a child told about the time her sister hid her favorite stuffed animal, she wrote, "Then my sister *perfadeed* me." Even though the student used the word as a verb when it is a noun, this is a meaning approximation that should be noticed and encouraged: "Wow! You used a new word from *The Tale of Despereaux*!"

As we all know from experience, you have to be brave to use a new word because you might not get it quite right at first. And just as with spelling, some children are more willing to take the risk and use new words than others. Encourage the more reluctant ones to be *courageous* and *adventurous* with words as they write.

Tip!

You can be encouraging and helpful at the same time. After complimenting a meaning approximation, it is fine during editing to explain how a new word is typically used and then to work with the child to reword a sentence using the word more conventionally.

When children first use words they've picked up from listening rather than reading, they sometimes think a phrase is a single word, like *per hour* as one word in this child's work: *Eagles can go 60 miles per hour.*

eagels can go 60 mris prowr.

Model Attention to Word Choice

All writers know what it means to labor over words. As I write this section, I'm thinking about how many times I've rewritten sentences in this book and changed the wording to convey important ideas more precisely. Word choice *matters*, but how do you teach this to children?

Do you write a morning message for your students, model writing new types of text, write shared class books, or class thank-you notes? You can model an attention to word choice basically any time you write in front of students. When you do, be sure to think out loud so students understand *why* you are choosing one word over another. Did you choose it because it is more precise? Has a different tone? Is a better fit for your audience?

A child uses literary language to describe a sky he saw on a camping trip: *It looked like orange sherbet.*

In addition to modeling, you can also teach children to think about word choice by encouraging them to:

Use words in interesting ways. Call attention to metaphors, similes, hyperbole, onomatopoeia, and idioms during read-alouds and then encourage children to try these in their writing.

Check the class's word collections to find words with similar meanings so children can be more precise in their writing.

Think about word connotations. Words that mean similar things may still *feel* very different. Maybe a character is asking for something, and a child is thinking about a more precise word for *ask*. Let's think about *request* or *demand* as possible options. These words feel very different. *Request* means to ask for something politely, while *demand* means to ask for something forcefully. The connotation of the word can make a big difference in a story.

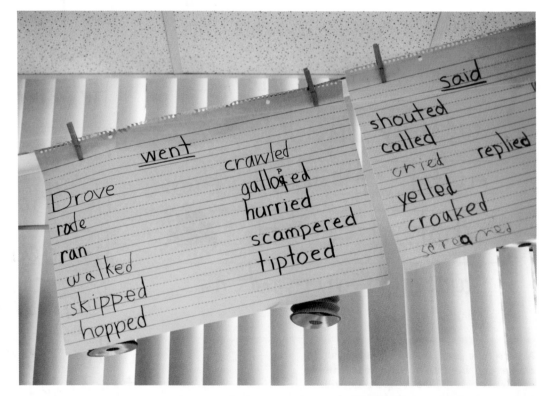

A chart in the room helps children think about more precise words for the common verbs *went* and *said*.

Notice how precise words such as *rustle* and *hustled* are in these sample pages from a child's chapter book about an encounter with a wolf.

Notice How Children Use Words

If we spend time thinking and talking about words—in read-alouds, in content-area learning, and in independent reading—we want to see children using those words in their writing. Now, some children will be more likely to use new words in their writing than others, but writing samples over time provide a window into the words that children know well enough to try to use.

Also, if you pay close attention to children's word choices in writing, you will find a great opportunity for formative assessment that can inform your instruction.

Consider questions like these as you look at children's writing:

Are there words I've been teaching that lots of children are using?

★ If you see this, consider what you did that might have made children feel confident to use these words. Can you replicate that?

Are there words I've been teaching that children don't seem confident to use (even though the writing context suggests them)?

★ If you see this, consider circling back around to these words. Perhaps you need to model again how to use them or coach some children one-on-one to use these words when it makes sense in their writing.

Would it be helpful to have this child (who is using new vocabulary) share their writing with the rest of the class?

★ Whenever you do see children using words you've taught, highlight this, and other children will often follow along.

Are children using interesting words that I *haven't* taught?

★ Have children share this writing as well and talk about how they came to know and use the interesting vocabulary. Be a class that celebrates words!

What other words could I teach because children *need* them to express their ideas?

★ Look for opportunities to share new words that children need to express their ideas. Children writing about their passion for toys that spin will be eager to learn all kinds of words, such as *rotate* and *revolve*!

7

The Beginning

inauguration dawning
inception opening
outset
commencement
kickoff
takeoff origin
opener source
starting point blast off
prelude
basis preface

The End...and the Beginning!

I hope that this book has offered you new ways to think about children's vocabulary development in your classroom as well as some concrete ideas to get started on Monday morning! Let's agree to stop thinking about vocabulary as a reading skill, as a component to master during a particular time of day, or as a list for children to memorize. Rather, let's think about learning words and using words as a crucial part of all of the learning that children do in our classrooms. I know that planning for this across-the-day vocabulary instruction may feel challenging at first, but rising to this challenge really does matter for children's learning. So, rather than the end of a book, let's think of this moment as a new beginning, a commencement, an opportunity to bring the power of words into your classroom. Now is the time to make a plan and get started!

Works Cited

Children's Literature References

Boothroyd, Jennifer. 2015. *What Is Severe Weather?* Minneapolis, MN: Lerner Publications.

Brown, Marcia. 1982. *Cinderella*. New York: Aladdin.

Church, E. B., and D. Ohanesian. 2010. *What's the Weather?* New York: Scholastic Children's Press.

Cobb, Vicki. 2003. *I Face the Wind*. New York: HarperCollins.

DiCamillo, Kate. 2009. *Mercy Watson to the Rescue*. Somerville, MA: Candlewick.

———. 2015. *The Tale of Despereaux: Being the Story of a Mouse, a Princess, Some Soup, and a Spool of Thread*. Somerville, MA: Candlewick.

Edison, Erin. 2012. *Clouds*. North Mankato, MN: Capstone.

Gibbons, Gail. 1984. *The Seasons of Arnold's Apple Tree*. New York: Houghton Mifflin Harcourt.

Henkes, Kevin. 1991. *Chrysanthemum*. New York: Greenwillow Books.

Johnson, Robin. 2013. *What Is Precipitation?* St. Catharines, Ontario: Crabtree.

Kalman, Bobbie. 2008. *Plants Are Living Things*. St. Catherines, Ontario: Crabtree.

Koscielniak, Bruce. 1995. *Geoffrey Groundhog Predicts the Weather*. Boston: Houghton Mifflin Harcourt.

MacAulay, Kelley. 2014. *How Do Plants Survive?* St. Catherines, Ontario: Crabtree.

Miller, Reagan. 2014. *Engineers Build Models*. St. Catherines, Ontario: Crabtree.

Mora, Pat. 2014. *Water Rolls, Water Rises / El agua rueda, el agua sube*. San Francisco: Children's Book Press.

Morgan, Emily. 2016. *Next Time You See a Cloud*. Arlington, VA: National Science Teachers Association.

O'Connor, Jane. 2009. *Fancy Nancy: Poison Ivy Expert*. New York: HarrperTrophy.

Pak, Soyung. 1999. *Dear Juno*. New York: Viking.

Reynolds, Peter H. 2018. *The Word Collector*. New York: Orchard Books.

Rosinsky, Natalie. 2003. *Light: Shadows, Mirrors, and Rainbows*. Minneapolis, MN: Picture Window Books.

Rotner, Shelley. 2017. *Hello Autumn!* New York: Holiday House.

Rotner, Shelley, and Sheila Kelly. 2015. *Families*. New York: Holiday House.

Shange, Ntozake. 1994. *I Live in Music*. New York: Steward, Tabori & Chang.

Snicket, Lemony. 1999. *The Reptile Room: Or, Murder!* A Series of Unfortunate Events No. 2. New York: HarperTrophy.

Stuart, Carrie. 2010. *Is It Hot or Cold?* New York: The Rosen Publishing Group.

White, E. B. 1952. *Charlotte's Web*. New York: HarperCollins.

Willems, Mo. 2010. *Knuffle Bunny Free: An Unexpected Diversion*. New York: HarperCollins / Balzer + Bray.

Research References

Baker, S., N. Lesaux, M. Jayanthi, J. Dimino, C. P. Proctor, J. Morris, R. Gersten, K. Haymond, M. J. Kieffer, S. Linan-Thompson, and R. Newman-Gonchar. 2014. *Teaching Academic Content and Literacy to English Learners in Elementary and Middle School* (NCEE 2014-4012). Washington, DC: National Center for Education Evaluation and Regional Assistance (NCEE), Institute of Education Sciences, U.S. Department of Education. https://ies.ed.gov/ncee/wwc/PracticeGuide/19.

Barber, J., and G. N. Cervetti. 2019. *No More Science Kits or Texts in Isolation*. Portsmouth, NH: Heinemann.

Beck, I. L., and M. G. McKeown. 1991. "Conditions of Vocabulary Acquisition." In *Handbook of Reading Research* Vol. 2, edited by R. Barr, M. L. Kamil, P. B. Mosenthal, and P. D. Pearson. Mahwah, NJ: Erlbaum.

Beck, I. L., M. G. McKeown, and L. Kucan. 2013. *Bringing Words to Life: Robust Vocabulary Instruction*. New York: Guilford Press.

Biemiller, A., and C. Boote. 2006. "An Effective Method for Building Meaning Vocabulary in Primary Grades." *Journal of Educational Psychology* 98(1): 44.

Carlisle, J. F., B. Kelcey, and D. Berebitsky. 2013. "Teachers' Support of Students' Vocabulary Learning During Literacy Instruction in High Poverty Elementary Schools." *American Educational Research Journal* 50(6): 1360–91.

Cervetti, G. N., and T. S. Wright. 2020. "The Role of Knowledge in Understanding and Learning from Text." In *Handbook of Reading Research, Volume V*, edited by E. B. Moje, P. Afflerbach, P. Enciso, and N. K. Lesaux, 237–60. New York: Routledge, Taylor, and Francis.

Cervetti, G. N., T. S. Wright, and H. Hwang. 2016. "Conceptual Coherence, Comprehension, and Vocabulary Acquisition: A Knowledge Effect?" *Reading and Writing* 29(4): 761–79.

Christian, K., F. J. Morrison, J. A. Frazier, and G. Massetti. 2000. "Specificity in the Nature and Timing of Cognitive Growth in Kindergarten and First Grade." *Journal of Cognition and Development* 1(4): 429–48.

Cobb, C., and C. Blachowicz. 2014. *No More "Look Up the List" Vocabulary Instruction*. Portsmouth, NH: Heinemann.

Cunningham, A. E., and K. E. Stanovich. 1991. "Tracking the Unique Effects of Print Exposure in Children: Associations with Vocabulary, General Knowledge, and Spelling." *Journal of Educational Psychology* 83(2): 264.

———. 1997. "Early Reading Acquisition and Its Relation to Reading Experience and Ability 10 Years Later." *Developmental Psychology* 33(6): 934.

Dickinson, D. K., and M. V. Porche. 2011. "Relation Between Language Experiences in Preschool Classrooms and Children's Kindergarten and Fourth-Grade Language and Reading Abilities." *Child Development* 82(3): 870–86.

Gotwals, A. W., and T. Wright. 2017. "From 'Plants Don't Eat' to 'Plants Are Producers': The Role of Vocabulary in Scientific Sense-Making." *Science and Children* 55(3): 44–50.

Greene Brabham, E., and C. Lynch-Brown. 2002. "Effects of Teachers' Reading-Aloud Styles on Vocabulary Acquisition and Comprehension of Students in the Early Elementary Grades." *Journal of Educational Psychology* 94(3): 465.

Marino, E. C. 2017. *Quantum Field Theory Approach to Condensed Matter Physics*. Cambridge, UK: Cambridge University Press.

Marulis, L. M., and S. B. Neuman. 2010. "The Effects of Vocabulary Intervention on Young Children's Word Learning: A Meta-Analysis." *Review of Educational Research* 80(3): 300–35.

McKeown, M. G. 1993. "Creating Effective Definitions for Young Word Learners." *Reading Research Quarterly* 28(1): 17–31.

McKeown, M. G., and I. L. Beck. 2014. "Effects of Vocabulary Instruction on Measures of Language Processing: Comparing Two Approaches." *Early Childhood Research Quarterly* 29(4): 520–30.

Michigan Department of Education. 2015. "Read Aloud with Attention to Vocabulary—Tanya S. Wright." May 27, 2015. YouTube video. www.youtube.com/watch?v=ynPdxVP4q4Y.

Michigan Virtual. 2017a. "K–3 Essential 2, Bullet 3: Vocabulary in Read Alouds Sample Video." December 1, 2017. YouTube video. https://youtu.be/8POsnXPWTxI.

———. 2017b. "K–3 Essential 2, Bullet 5: Instructional Strategies During Read Alouds Sample Video." December 1, 2017. YouTube video. www.youtube.com/watch?v=W9VTZaCeqMg&feature=youtu.be.

———. 2018a. "K–3 Essential 7, Bullet 5: Morphology Sample Video." August 24, 2018. YouTube video. www.youtube.com/watch?v=fP74wNkJZ34&feature=youtu.be.

———. 2018b. "Pre-K Essential 3, Bullets 2 & 3: Interactive Read-Alouds and Vocabulary Development Sample Video." October 17, 2018. YouTube video. www.youtube.com/watch?v=5ru9inVl-v4&feature=youtu.be.

Miller, G. A., and P. M. Gildea. 1987. "How Children Learn Words." *Scientific American* 257(3): 94–99.

Nagy, W., and D. Townsend. 2012. "Words as Tools: Learning Academic Vocabulary as Language Acquisition." *Reading Research Quarterly* 47(1): 91–108.

Neugebauer, S. R., P. B. Gámez, M. D. Coyne, I. T. Cólon, D. B. McCoach, and S. Ware. 2017. "Promoting Word Consciousness to Close the Vocabulary Gap in Young Word Learners." *The Elementary School Journal* 118(1): 28–54.

Neuman, S. B., and J. Dwyer. 2009. "Missing in Action: Vocabulary Instruction in Pre-K." *The Reading Teacher* 62(5): 384–92.

Neuman, S. B., and T. S. Wright. 2014. "The Magic of Words: Teaching Vocabulary in the Early Childhood Classroom." *American Educator* 38(2): 4–13. www.aft.org/periodical/american-educator/summer-2014/magic-words.

O'Connor, R. E., H. L. Swanson, and C. Geraghty. 2010. "Improvement in Reading Rate Under Independent and Difficult Text Levels: Influences on Word and Comprehension Skills." *Journal of Educational Psychology* 102(1): 1–19.

Ouellette, G. P. 2006. "What's Meaning Got to Do With It: The Role of Vocabulary in Word Reading and Reading Comprehension." *Journal of Educational Psychology* 98(3): 554.

Paris, S. G. 2005. "Reinterpreting the Development of Reading Skills." *Reading Research Quarterly* 40(2): 184–202.

Recht, D. R., and L. Leslie. 1988. "Effect of Prior Knowledge on Good and Poor Readers' Memory of Text." *Journal of Educational Psychology* 80(1): 16.

Scott, J. A., and W. E. Nagy. 1997. "Understanding the Definitions of Unfamiliar Verbs." *Reading Research Quarterly* 32(2): 184–200.

Shanahan, T., K. Callison, C. Carriere, N. K. Duke, P. D. Pearson, C. Schatschneider, and J. Torgesen. 2010. *Improving Reading Comprehension in Kindergarten Through 3rd Grade: A Practice Guide* (NCEE 2010-4038). Washington, DC: U.S. Department of Education, National Center for Education Evaluation and Regional Assistance, Institute of Education Sciences. https://ies.ed.gov/ncee/wwc/PracticeGuide/14.

Skibbe, L. E., C. M. Connor, F. J. Morrison, and A. M. Jewkes. 2011. "Schooling Effects on Preschoolers' Self-Regulation, Early Literacy, and Language Growth." *Early Childhood Research Quarterly* 26(1): 42–49.

SOLID Start. 2020. *SOLID Start Curriculum: Weather Forecasting Unit*. Michigan State University College of Education. http://solidstart.msu.edu.

Stahl, S. A., and M. M. Fairbanks. 1986. "The Effects of Vocabulary Instruction: A Model-Based Meta-Analysis." *Review of Education Research* 56(1): 72–110.

Sternberg, R. 1987. "Most Vocabulary Is Learned from Context." In *The Nature of Vocabulary Acquisition*, edited by M. McKeown and M. Curtiss, 89–105. Hillsdale, NJ: Erlbaum.

Swanborn, M. S., and K. De Glopper. 1999. "Incidental Word Learning While Reading: A Meta-Analysis." *Review of Educational Research* 69(3): 261–85.

Varelas, M., and C. C. Pappas. 2006. "Intertextuality in Read-Alouds of Integrated Science-Literacy Units in Urban Primary Classrooms: Opportunities for the Development of Thought and Language." *Cognition and Instruction* 24(2): 211–59.

Weizman, Z. O., and C. E. Snow. 2001. "Lexical Output as Related to Children's Vocabulary Acquisition: Effects of Sophisticated Exposure and Support for Meaning." *Developmental Psychology* 37(2): 265.

Wise, C. N. 2019. "Assessment and Instruction for Developing Second Graders' Skill in Ascertaining Word Meanings from Context." PhD diss., University of Michigan.

Wright, T. S. 2014. "From Potential to Reality: Content-Rich Vocabulary and Informational Text." *The Reading Teacher* 67(5): 359–67.

———. 2019. "Reading to Learn from the Start: The Power of Interactive Read-Alouds." *American Educator* 42(4). www.aft.org/ae/winter2018-2019/wright.

Wright, T. S., and G. N. Cervetti. 2017. "A Systematic Review of the Research on Vocabulary Instruction That Impacts Text Comprehension." *Reading Research Quarterly* 52(2): 203–26.

Wright, T. S., and A. W. Gotwals. 2017a. "Supporting Disciplinary Talk from the Start of School: Teaching Students to Think and Talk Like Scientists." *The Reading Teacher* 71(2): 189–97.

———. 2017b. "Supporting Kindergartners' Science Talk in the Context of an Integrated Science and Disciplinary Literacy Curriculum." *The Elementary School Journal* 117(3): 513–37.

Wright, T. S., C. Haverly, J. West, and A. W. Gotwals. 2019. "Discussion Supports Sense-Making Within and Across Lessons." *Science and Children* 57(4): 50–56.

Wright, T. S., and S. B. Neuman. 2013. "Vocabulary Instruction in Commonly Used Kindergarten Core Reading Curricula." *The Elementary School Journal* 113(3): 386–408.

———. 2014. "Paucity and Disparity in Kindergarten Oral Vocabulary Instruction." *Journal of Literacy Research* 46(3): 330–57.